ESSAYS AND STUDIES
1980

ESSAYS AND STUDIES
1980

BEING VOLUME THIRTY-THREE OF THE NEW SERIES
OF ESSAYS AND STUDIES COLLECTED FOR
THE ENGLISH ASSOCIATION

BY INGA-STINA EWBANK

JOHN MURRAY

FIFTY ALBEMARLE STREET LONDON

*Set, printed and bound in Great Britain by
Fakenham Press Limited, Fakenham, Norfolk*

0 7195 3745 2

Preface

THERE are many kinds of collector's pleasure—none perhaps keener than that conveyed by John Heminges and Henry Condell, who put together the first collected edition of Shakespeare's plays. Yet, in their Preface 'To the Great Variety of Readers' they also felt that 'it is not our province, who only gather his works and give them to you, to praise him'. Taking a leaf out of their great book, I do not presume to praise the contents of the present volume. I wish, however, to thank the English Association for making me its collector. The collector of a volume of *Essays and Studies* has the particular pleasure—not altogether unrelated to that experienced by the subjects of that popular TV programme called 'This Is Your Life'—of seeing some of his friends—past and present colleagues, teachers and pupils—gathered within a single cover. But, as previous volumes show, that (possibly selfish) pleasure does not preclude a timeless and general value in the collection as a contribution to the study of English. It is to be hoped that this, the thirty-third volume in the series, proves the rule without being an exception.

In this case, seven friends were asked to contribute an essay, and all kindly complied, despite my temerity of asking that they write on English drama, of any period. In the end, as befits the Golden Age of English Drama, the Renaissance came to be best represented, with three essays out of seven dealing with drama composed between the coming of Shakespeare and the closing of the theatres in 1642. Furthermore, Stanley Wells's essay on Leigh Hunt's theatre criticism not only bridges the Renaissance and Romantic periods but also invites us to hear Leigh Hunt 'talking to other times'. But the chronological scope of the volume as a whole stretches from G. C. Britton's exploration of speech and character in some late medieval plays to Kenneth Muir's presentation of a perhaps unfairly neglected twentieth-century dramatist. Within the chronological scope, certain continuities of concern have, naturally enough, developed: concern with the relationship between word and vision in the theatre, or between tradition and individual talent. G. K. Hunter deals with the visual 'language' of the Elizabethan theatre, and John Dixon Hunt demonstrates the cross-fertilization between ideas about gardens and ideas about theatres in the seventeenth and eighteenth centuries. In their separate ways, Anne Barton's and Jonathan Dollimore's essays show how a dramatist's vision will shape his technique and the structure of his plays. Altogether, in its variety of critical approaches, the volume addresses itself to anyone interested in the study of English literature. The collector's hope for the volume, then, must be, like Heminges and Condell's, that the reader 'will find enough, both to draw, and hold you'.

Bedford College,   Inga-Stina Ewbank
University of London
December 1979

Contents

I LANGUAGE AND CHARACTER IN SOME LATE
MEDIEVAL PLAYS   1
G. C. Britton

II FLATCAPS AND BLUECOATS: VISUAL SIGNALS
ON THE ELIZABETHAN STAGE   16
G. K. Hunter

III MARSTON'S 'ANTONIO' PLAYS AND SHAKESPEARE'S
'TROILUS AND CRESSIDA': THE BIRTH OF A
RADICAL DRAMA   48
Jonathan Dollimore

IV OXYMORON AND THE STRUCTURE OF FORD'S
'THE BROKEN HEART'   70
Anne Barton

V THEATRES, GARDENS, AND GARDEN-THEATRES   95
John Dixon Hunt

VI SHAKESPEARE IN LEIGH HUNT'S THEATRE
CRITICISM   119
Stanley Wells

VII THE PLAYS OF GORDON BOTTOMLEY
Kenneth Muir   139

I

Language and Character in some Late Medieval Plays

G. C. BRITTON

In their introduction to *World and Child*, Schell and Schuchter comment that the author 'seems to have been the first to have sufficient verbal facility to make his hero's diction change as he lives through the ages of his life. He speaks flat narrative verse as an infant—perhaps the equivalent of no speech at all. As a child he babbles in fluent Childish. As a young man he utters love lyrics, as an adult the alliterative bombastic vaunting of the King of Life and of the Herods and Pilates in the mystery plays. As an old man he whines out his complaint.'[1]

One would not wish to deny that the language of the 'mankind' character, who progresses in the course of the play from infancy to old age, differs from one stage to another, and that the differences are significant. In fact, one could go farther, and point out that the language also differs between one character and another, but since these characters often merely reflect the different states of the mankind character himself, as he progresses from Infans via Wanton, Lust-and-Lykyng, Manhood and Shame, to Age, this would only be to say the same thing in a different form. We have to resist any implication that the playwright is more interested in the development of the character of an individual than in the portrayal of allegorical or semi-allegorical figures, states and types.

[1] E. T. Schell and J. D. Schuchter eds., *English Morality Plays and Moral Interludes* (New York, 1969), 167–8. Both titles, *The World and the Child* and *Mundus et Infans*, appear on Wynkyn de Worde's title-page of 1522. Reference below is to the text in J. M. Manly's *Specimens of Pre-Shaksperean Drama*, Vol. I (Boston, 1897), 353–85 (the line numbering differs from that of Schell and Schuchter). Manly, correctly in my opinion, divides the text into stanzas. The play is also available in Tudor Facsimile Texts, No. 135.

But we must not fall into the modern error that there is therefore a mechanical transference of abstract moral or theological thinking into dramatic-allegorical terms, for in the middle ages, in literature at least, it is doubtful whether one can talk of abstract qualities in divorce from actual examples, real or imagined. In *World and Child* Conscience *is* a friar, and in the cycle plays Abraham *is* Faith. This may account for the uncomfortable feeling that we now sometimes get in reading medieval non-dramatic as well as dramatic works: that there is a conflict between verisimilitude and an intrusive didacticism. We are dealing, however, with a question of character function rather than character portrayal; the character is defined at the appropriate time by language that is appropriate to the function rather than to the individual who is uttering it. The function must be immediately apparent, and we are often aware from the first speech of a character in a late medieval play what we are meant to think of his purpose and place in the thematic pattern, developed or developing. We gather this not only from what he says but also from the way in which he says it. Further, we must not be surprised if his language from time to time (but not in every play) shows a shift in his function inconsistent with the demands of individual characterization, but entirely consistent with the demands of the exposition of the play's didactic theme. It would seem true to say that, far from being original in his use of language, the author of *World and Child* is drawing heavily, if cleverly, on an established tradition. It is interesting also that he seems to be beginning to develop, consciously or subconsciously, that tradition in the direction of the exposition of individual character, a development that may be seen elsewhere too.

The use of that tradition is clear from the first entrance of Mundus, who uses the typical boastful language, highly alliterative, that we associate with the 'tyrant' character of the cycle plays:[1]

> Syrs, seace of your sawes, what-so befall,
> And loke ye bow bonerly to my byddynge,

[1] He is, of course, found outside the cycle plays too; see the beginning of *Pride of Life*.

> For I am ruler of realmes, I warne you all,
> And ouer all fodys I am kynge.
>
> (1–4)

He goes on in the next twenty lines to proclaim his power, how he is lord of horses and places, what his name is, how he must be obeyed, or poverty will follow:

> I am a kynge in euery case;
> Me thynketh I am a god of grace
> The floure of vertue foloweth me.
>
> (19–21)

He sits 'semely in se', and calls all to follow him.

This is a clever variation on the kind of speech that we find as the opening of the Towneley *Pharoah* (1–24), the simplest form of the conventional tyrant opening, where Pharoah calls for quiet, proclaims his power, threatens hanging and drawing (not poverty) to those who disobey him, and promises peace (not riches) to those who obey. The claim to be god is missing, and we shall have to take this up below. The passing claim to beauty ('semely' 12, 22) will also recur more clearly stated. The tyrant character is always attached in the cycles to biblical and historical characters of worldly power, such as Pharoah, Caesar Augustus, Octavian, and most notably Herod and Pilate. The fact that Mundus is historically unlocated, a character as king, indeed, but unspecific, with strong allegorical traits, tells us on reflection as much about the nature of the worldly tyrant of the cycle play as about Mundus himself, for the very possibility of such close comparison reveals the allegorical element in the character. The anachronisms common in the cycle plays show that there is a sense in which the plays are not located in a specific time, but have perpetual application. The point should not be lost sight of even when, as for example in both Towneley and York Pilates, some process of individualization, or at least of narrowing to a more closely characterized role, takes place. An interesting variation on the tyrant which demonstrates the shift of function mentioned above is to be found in the Chester *Annunciation and Nativity*, where

Octavian first enters (line 185) as a tyrant, even having two
stanzas in French to back up the point. Two senators enter, 'sent
from all Rome' to offer him the kind of submission that he has up
to now been demanding, but with the important addition 'as God
to honour thee'. Octavian's tone immediately changes to one of
rationality entirely out of accord with a tyrant character as he
explains why he cannot accept the attribution of godhead, and we
pass to the thematically important Sybilline prophecy of the
coming of the King of kings. It is clear that though Octavian's
'character' differs in an important way from the tyrant, the playwright contemplates no alternative way to introduce him as a
figure of worldly power. He is not primarily interested in the
consistency of characterization of Octavian as an individual. The
emperor has a function which goes outside that.

The entrance of Infans is in marked contrast with that of
Mundus, and draws upon another tradition of opening speeches:

> Cryst, our kynge, graunte you clerly to know the case!
> To meue of this mater that is in my mynde,
> Clerely (to) declare it Cryst graunte me grace!
>
> (25-7)

As opposed to Mundus's threats, his address to the audience is in
the nature of a prayer, and introduces, as such prayers do, a piece
of exposition. We are reminded of such characters as Contem-
placio in the N-town plays. There, in play 8, lines 1-8 are prayer
and exhortation to the players to be clear in speech, 9-16 is an
outline of action, 17-25 a prayer for the audience; the exposition
is in formal language, laced with Latin vocabulary. Such formal
and latinate language is characteristic of expository passages. God
himself opens the Chester cycle with fifty lines of alliterative,
aureate, even macaronic statement, though latinate language does
not, as we might at first think, belong to him by nature but by his
dramatic function here. His speech of anger at lines 214-29 is
hardly latinate at all. It is interesting that both speeches in their
different ways are more controlled, less repetitive, than introduc-
tory or angry speeches by tyrants.

Another weighty and latinate introduction is delivered by Mercy at the beginning of *Mankind*, 1–44, and in fact Mischief makes fun of him in his reply by parodying Mercy's diction.[1] In *World and Child*, however, there is an important compromise with verisimilitude for although Infans's speech is formal it is simple in vocabulary. This is, no doubt, what leads Schell and Schuchter to talk of the 'flat narrative verse' he speaks as an infant.[2] Interestingly enough, they add that it is 'perhaps the equivalent of no speech at all', for, of course (though this is not what they mean), the speech is virtually the equivalent of a prologue in which certain necessary things are established, including not only the moral and didactic but also the dramatic context of the action that is to follow. This prologue is out of dramatic time, and ends with a bridge passage in which both antagonists are brought together: the universality of the action that is to follow is thereby established. The movement from one stage to the next is clearly established by the change from a formal to an attempt at a naturalistic kind of speech (what Schell and Schuchter happily call 'fluent childish'):

> Gramercy, Worlde, for myne araye!
> For now I purpose me to playe...
>
> A ha! Wanton is my name!
> I can many a quaynte game:
> Lo, my toppe I dryue in same,—
>   Se, it torneth rounde!
> I can with my scorge-stycke
> My felowe vpon the heed hytte,
> And wyghtly from hym make a skyppe,
>   And blere on hym my tonge.
>
>   (72–83)

---

[1] On the significance of this, see P. Neuss, 'Active and idle language: dramatic images in *Mankind*', *Medieval Drama*, ed. N. Denny, Stratford-upon-Avon Studies 16 (London, 1973), 41–67, esp. 46.

[2] Though it is doubtful whether such a term is justly appropriate to such lovely lines as 'Fourty wekes I was frely fedde/Within my moders wombe;/Full oft of dethe she was adred/Whan that I sholde parte her from' (40–43).

The importance of the stanza patterns established by Manly is immediately apparent: they match the nature of the language being used. The change of stanza at, for example, the beginning of *Mankind* could be shown to be equally significant. The whole of Wanton's speech not only describes childish attitudes, but echoes them in the language. It will be noticed however that description (not portrayal) is the key to what is being said. At the end of this speech, Wanton leaves this style in order to point the transition to the next stage of the action. Although he is still Wanton, he no longer sounds like Wanton:

> But, syrs, whan I was seuen yere of age,
> I was sent to the Worlde to take wage,
> And this seuen yere I haue ben his page
>   And kept his commaundement.
> Now I wyll wende to the Worlde, that worthy emperour.
> Hayle, lorde of grete honour!
> This vij yere I haue serued you in hall and in boure
>   With all my trewe entent.
>
> (115–22)

The radical change of mode of speech indicating shift of function is more easily paralleled in good characters than in the tyrant. Three examples, all from the Towneley cycle, will do to show the phenomenon. First of all, Noah acts as 'expositor', using appropriately dignified language, in the first seventy-two lines of his play. The exposition is continued by God himself, and in conversation between the two, until line 182. The language change between the dialogue of God and Noah and the dialogue of Noah and his wife is striking, not simply from formal to colloquial but from dignified to scabrous. Although the complex stanza form is maintained, many of the stanzas are disintegrated into short pieces of dialogue. After a brief descriptive piece of the making of the ark, the dialogue style recurs and dominates, though not quite exclusively; note especially lines 343–51, where Noah is used in an apparently descriptive stanza to make a point about the breakdown of universal order that is reflected in his own quarrel with his wife:

> Behold to the heuen the cataractes all,
> That are open full euen grete and small,
> And the planettis seuen left has thare stall,
> Thise thoners and levyn downe gar fall
> > ffull stout,
> Both halles and bowers,
> Castels and towres;
> ffull sharp ar thise showers,
> > that renys aboute;
>
> Therfor, wife, haue done com into ship fast.
> *Vxor* Yei, noe, go cloute thi shone the better will thai last.
> *Prima mulier* Good moder, com in sone ffor all is ouer cast,
> Both the son and the mone.
>
> > (343-55)

... and so on. Thus the explicative style does not belong to Noah only when he is in conversation with God. It is introduced whenever the theme demands it, and, in fact, when the seven stars are restored, it is Mrs Noah, hardly in her character as it has so far been shown to us, that makes the comment. Her two lines are not even at first sight obviously connected with what has gone before:

> *Noe* We will do as ye bid vs we will no more be wroth,
> > Dere barnes!
> Now to the helme will I hent,
> And to my ship tent.
> *Vxor* I se on the firmament,
> Me thynk, the seven starnes.
>
> > (418-23)

From this point on there is no further attempt to characterize Noah and Mrs Noah, either as individuals or as traditional opponents in the eternal war between men and women. Henceforth they share the explicative function by which the playwright gives point to his play.

A second example of shift of function is to be found in the Towneley *Salutation*, where the language changes from that of colloquy between two pregnant kinswomen asking after each other's health to a didactic passage (49–78) beginning 'Magnificat anima mea dominum'. Having delivered this weighty speech, Mary moves without pause into 'Well, my dear, I'll have to be off now':

> Elezabeth, myn awnt dere
> My lefe I take at you here
> ffor I dwell now full lang.
>
> (79–81)

To the modern ear, the effect is likely to be one of bathos. Finally, we may notice how the Wakefield Master exploits this facility of immediate shift in order to achieve a most touching effect in the 'Hail' stanzas of the *Second Shepherds' Play*, e.g.

> *Primus pastor* Hayll, comly and clene, hayll, yong child!
>   hayll, maker, as I meyne, of a madyn so mylde!
>   Thou has waryd, I weyne, the warlo so wylde;
>   The fals gyler of teyn now goys he begylde.
>   lo, he merys;
>   lo, he laghys, my swetyng,
>   A welfare metyng,
>   I haue holden my hetyng;
>   haue a bob of cherys.
>
> (710–18)

Wanton has moved across the place, then, to address Mundus again in his formal stanza and language, quite unlike 'fluent childish'. Mundus replies in his alliterative style, and changes Wanton's name to Lust-and-Lykyng:

> A ha! now Lust and Lykyng is my name!
>   I am as fresshe as flourys in Maye;
>   I am semely shapen in same,
>   And proudely apperelde in garmentes gaye.
>
> (131–4)

The cycle plays, of course, offer no parallel to the 'young lover', though Herod in the Towneley *Magi* claims to be a lover (31–6), and in York and N-town to be a beauty. It is perhaps not without significance that Absolom who played Herod upon a scaffold high (*Canterbury Tales* A3384) was both a dandy and an aspiring lover. That there was an established young-lover character one suspects from the first of the Reynes Extracts (A Speech of 'Delight'), with which its first editor compared this very speech.[1] The aureate vocabulary of the Reynes Extract is rather appropriate to the tyrant, whereas Lust-and-Lykyng's vocabulary is much simpler, with a slight flavour of conventional love poetry. It is worth noting that though Lust-and-Lykyng has only thirteen lines *in propria persona*, the playwright feels it worth while to introduce a new stanza form, returning him to the old stanza when he turns to the audience in an explanatory-narrative passage (144–51).

Mundus, though 'characterized' himself by his tyrant language, has actually been a mere background to Infans in his various manifestations. Now, again, changing Lust-and-Lykyng's name to Manhood, he proceeds in the 'expository' stanza to list the 'seven kings', the Deadly Sins, that follow him. Manhood takes immediately to Pride in a divided stanza that imitates conversation. He promises

> That I shall truely Pryde present
> I swere by Saynt Thomas of Kent;
> To serue hym truely is myn entent,
>   With mayne and all my myght.
>
> (192–5)

In a whole stanza, Mundus 'arrays him new in robes royal', dubs him knight, exhorts him to practise chivalry, gives him

> grace and also beaute,
> Gold and syluer, gret plente,
> Of the wronge to make the ryght.
>
> (201–3)

[1] See I. G. Calderhead, 'Morality fragments from Norfolk', *MP*, 14 (1916), 1–9. The latest edition is by N. Davis in *Non-Cycle Plays and Fragments*, E.E.T.S., S.S.1 (London, 1970). The tradition must be older; cf. the Squire in the *General Prologue*, for whom Chaucer may owe a debt to the portrait of Mirth in the *Roman de la Rose*.

The ambivalence of line 203 is obvious enough. The response of Manhood is significantly reminiscent of the 'Hail' stanzas that come near the end of the Shepherds' Plays of the Towneley and N-town cycles. The clear implication is that the worship that belongs to the Lord of Life is being given to Mundus:

> Gramercy, Worlde and emperour!
> Gramercy, Worlde and governoure!
> Gramercy, comforte in all coloure!
>   And now I take my leue, fare-well!
>
> (204–20)

Mundus completes the stanza with his farewell, and Manhood seems to take a position elsewhere in the place. Mundus remains behind and makes his last speech. In view of the play's title, it seems strange that this should happen not a quarter of the way through it. By comparison, the *Castle of Perseverance* shows the possibility offered by keeping the World in contention for Mankind's soul until the last. But the author of *World and Child* is making a psychological point of some subtlety in allowing Mundus to depart from the scene so soon,[1] a point he makes clear almost entirely by exploiting the language convention.

First of all, we are reminded of Mundus's tyrant character by a spectacular display of alliterative pyrotechnics:

> Lo, syrs, I am a prynce, peryllous y provyde,
>   I-preuyd full peryllous and pethely i-pyght,
> As a lorde in eche londe I am belouyd;
>   Myne eyen do shyne as lanterne bryght;
>
> I am a creature comely, out of care;
>   Empereours and kynges they knele to my kne;
> Euery man is a-ferde whan I do on hym stare,
>   For all mery medell-erthe maketh mencyon of me.
>
> (216–23)

---

[1] It also makes it possible for the actor playing Mundus to double his part— no trivial consideration!

All these are standard characteristics, and all are paralleled in the cycle *Magi* plays.[1] Like Herod in the N-town *Magi*, Mundus is richly dressed (232), and, as in Towneley, a lady's man (234). But the apex of his claim is in 224–7, where he usurps the position of the Creator: 'Yet all is my hande-werke, both by downe and by dale', etc. The obvious parallel would be Lucifer, but this element occurs too in the Herod of the *Magi* plays.[2] In N-town he says, 'Ffor both of hevyn and of herth I am king sertayn' (8), in Chester he is master of the devils, mankind, the moon, the sun and the rain (175–85), and in York he adds a few Roman gods for good measure (1–14). (In Towneley he is Mahomet's man, a feature that occurs elsewhere too.) Mundus's whole speech shows him to belong more specifically to the Herod tradition than broadly to the tyrant tradition. The reason is obvious enough: Mundus is to be shown as in specific opposition to Christ, as Herod is too (he is called 'King of kings' in Chester and Towneley). The light is reflected back on to Herod himself, for, as it is hardly possible to call Mundus an entirely allegorical character, so it is not possible to see Herod as an individual.

It is, one hopes, not entirely irrelevant to digress at this point to show how the problem of what to do with these characters who are anchored in history on the one hand, but on the other have their thematic function to perform in the play, is highlighted by the difficulties the cycle playwrights have with Pilate. Though they are less striking than in the case of the Chester Octavian, problems of inconsistency inevitably occur. The cycle playwrights solve these problems in various ways. York simply ignores them, rant and reason being unreconciled. Towneley makes Pilate a treacherous hypocrite, presenting a reasonable face to Jesus while planning his downfall. Chester makes him, less interestingly, an out-and-out tyrant, but N-town resists the temptation to make him a tyrant at all, thus at one and the same time simplifying the opposition between the two antagonistic groups and making

[1] Except that in Chester Herod makes no claim to beauty.
[2] As we have seen above, Octavian rejects godhead in the Chester *Nativity* (ll. 297–306). In the Towneley *Talents* Pilate calls himself *dominus dominorum* (l. 10).

Pilate a kind of independent judge between the two. The effect is not lost even when Pilate gets angry in N-town at the news of the resurrection, for by then he has become the colonial governor protecting his position—an addition to our understanding of his character rather than a denial of what we have already seen. The N-town solution is probably the most appealing to the modern reader, but one wonders whether York is not more in conformity with medieval dramatic convention. The interesting sign is that the Towneley playwright felt so strongly about the conflict between the historical character and the temporally unlocated tyrant that he tried to reconcile the two.

Mundus's final stanza (228–36) is extended from the *abab* quatrain of four-stress lines with an added five-line two-stress pattern, *cdddc*. We are not told what now happens to him. There is little doubt that so far he has remained in the booth in which we see him sitting on the title-page of Wynkyn de Worde's print.[1] Meanwhile Infans under his various names has carried on his activities in the playing area, approaching the booth when required. Manly evidently pictures something of the sort, witness his suggested directions at lines 119 and 151: *He* [Infans] *approaches Mundus.* Now Mundus must vacate his booth; in fact, he must leave the playing area altogether, for he no longer has any function there, and the editors are undoubtedly right in supplying the stage direction *Exit.*

Manhood now addresses the audience in tyrant terms very similar to those earlier used by Mundus. His speech extends from 237 to 287, the longest speech in the play other than Perseveraunce's crucial oration that is finally to change Age's name to Repentance. Southern (p. 129) would divide the play into five 'Episodes', 1–287 being the first, and there is much to be said for this. Nevertheless, the two major climaxes in the play are marked by these two major speeches.[2] An itemization of the speech will

---

[1] See Tudor Facsimile Texts 135; also R. Southern, *The Staging of Plays before Shakespeare* (London, 1973), 128. Southern deals with the staging of the play on 126–42.

[2] A third long speech (ll. 787–810) of narrative summary and explication is given to Age near the beginning of the final 'Episode' or movement. He is now to be rescued from his predicament by Perseveraunce.

show a strong family resemblance to the customary Herod speech, even to the extent of sometimes hitting off the same words. He calls for quiet; he is a stout lord of all lands; no baron is bolder or brighter of complexion; he has power over far lands and all call him Manhood; he names the countries he has conquered; no emperor dares oppose him; he has injured or killed many men, and many ladies have loved him; no one is comparable with him:

> I am worthy and wyght, wytty and wyse,
> I am ryall arayde to reuen vnder the ryse,
> I am proudely aparelde in purpure and byse,
>   As golde I glyster in gere;
> I am styffe, stronge, stalworthe and stoute,
> I am the ryallest redely that renneth in this route,
> There is no knyght so grysly that I drede nor dout,
>   For I am so doughtly dyght ther may no dint me dere.
>   (267-74)

The Kings of the Seven Deadly Sins support him:

> Where is now so worthy a wyght?—
>   A wyght?
> Ye, as a wyght wytty,
> Here in this sete sytte I;
> For no loues lette I
>   Here for to sytte.
>   (282-7)

Mundus's claim to creatorship is not echoed, but the 'Seven Kings' who followed him now follow Manhood. The opening stanza arrangement bears a strong resemblance to that of Mundus's final speech: two alternately rhyming four-stress quatrains, followed by another (*abab*) and five two-stress lines (*cdddc*); then two more quatrains and another five-line piece. At the end are two octets, rather like heavy tail-rhyme stanzas, which echo the form of Mundus's speech of the Seven Kings, 168-84, neatly finished off by the six lines quoted above. The whole is highly alliterative. As his style of speech as well as its content and his action in taking Mundus's seat all show, Manhood is now completely identified with Mundus, a worldly tyrant-figure in his turn also identified, by his traditional style of speech, with Christ's arch-enemy. Dramatically there is no longer anything for Mundus *per se* to do; the 'mundus' character is still on stage, but he himself has been replaced by Manhood.

Future changes in Manhood, via Shame to Age, will also involve his using language of appropriate established styles. In his exchanges with Conscience, for example, he uses the undignified language of abuse that belongs not only to the tyrant but to that strange and scurrilous 'Garcio' character that crops up from time to time in medieval drama. His reaction to Conscience's rejection of wrath is in the language of wrath, e.g.

> Fye on the, fals flatterynge frere!
> Thou shalte rewe the tyme that thou came here;
> The deuyll mote set the on a fyre,
>   That euer I with the mete!

$$(401-4)$$

To introduce himself as Folly's man he is given a stanza trivial in style and rhythm:

> Now I wyll folowe Folye,
>   For Folye is my man;
> Ye, Folye is my felowe
>   And hath gyuen me a name:
> Conscyence called me Manhode,
>   Folye calleth me Shame.

$$(700-5)$$

As Age, his speech of regret (767 ff.), recalling what has gone before and drawing a moral, is in the formal, highly alliterative expository style; it concludes with lyric stanzas that draw upon the tradition of poems on the themes of 'ubi sunt' and 'signs of age'.[1] Space permits no further discussion, which would in fact increase only instances and not principles.

[1] But it is noticeable that the doctrinal lines 854–67 addressed by Perseveraunce not to the audience but as an exhortation to Manhood (or Age) are neither alliterative nor more latinate than is necessary to convey the subject matter. Is this perhaps a concession to verisimilitude in dialogue?

The more one looks at *World and Child*, the more one finds to say in favour of the playwright's skills. Not the least of these is his ability to vary his language in appropriate ways, but it would be a mistake to regard him as a thorough innovator in this field. His appropriate languages are appropriate because they have already been established as such in earlier work. In the cycle plays we can see them persisting in living performance up to and beyond the date of *World and Child*. It seems clear that, along with others of his time, he is moving character portrayal away from medieval towards Elizabethan ideas, though in fact the kind of play that *World and Child* is considerably limits him in what he can do in this way. It is perhaps that very fact that causes him to throw light on the technique of both his predecessors and his successors. Something has been said above of the older tradition. That older tradition of what has been there called (if rather unsatisfactorily) character function rather than character portrayal continues into later drama, often giving rise to descriptive, narrative and commentative passages which cause embarrassment to the modern producer and actor. Some of the most important, if not the longest, of such speeches are spoken by dramatically neutral characters, for example Second Lord, who may correspond to Nuntius or Explicator in the earlier plays. When spoken by a major character, one suspects that they are not necessarily to be taken, except incidentally or by implication, as revelatory of individual character.

II

Flatcaps and Bluecoats: Visual Signals on the Elizabethan Stage

G. K. HUNTER

THE etymology of the word *theatre* tells us that this is a place for using our eyes, for seeing things. The etymology of the word *auditorium* tells us the opposite, that here is a place for hearing. But no one feels the slightest discomfort at going to a play in a *theatrical auditorium*, for we are all well aware that plays make demands on both eyes and ears. The modern *spectator* seems, however, to be led by his eyes more than his ears and the modern 'media', film and television, increasingly subordinate words to images. It is commonly supposed that in Shakespeare's age the boot was on the other organ. The *spectator* (or *viewer* as some now prefer) of Shakespeare was then the *auditor*, and the dramatist as poet was said to secure his attention by wholly verbal means: to 'call the banished auditor home and tie His ear (with golden chains) to his melody'.[1] There is a certain snobbery in this of course. The ideology of the time did not support any clear sense of superiority in the visual. It was not only the conservative Ben Jonson who in his controversy with Inigo Jones rated words as the soul of drama, and spectacle as, well, mere spectacle.[2] The populace-pleasing Thomas Heywood sees the relationship of the two modes in the same way. In his *Londini Speculum* (1637) he speaks of 'Antic gesticulations, dances, and other mimic postures, devised only for the vulgar who are better delighted with that

[1] Dekker, *If This Be Not a Good Play, the Devil is in it* (1612); Prologue, ll. 31–2.

[2] See D. J. Gordon, 'Poet and architect: the intellectual setting of the quarrel between Ben Jonson and Inigo Jones', J.W.C.I. XII (1949), 152–78.

The author wishes to thank the John Simon Guggenheim Foundation for generous support in the period when this article was being revised.

which pleaseth the eyes than contenteth the ear'.[1] The slighting comments of both these authors are related, of course, to quasi-theatrical events outside the theatre proper, to situations where the threat of the spectacular was presumably more pressing. The public stage does not seem to have raised the competition to any such fervency: and indeed its physical conditions were such as to damp down any tendency to exalt sight at the expense of sound. The actors seem to have moved in a similar style of costumes and at the same level of lighting as the spectators; and the lighting, coming from heaven, could not be raised or lowered in response to the play. Scenery was exiguous and simple, stage machinery was rudimentary. On the other hand the language of the Elizabethan play (unlike that of the modern media) was often dazzlingly brilliant, composed with an elaboration that demanded concentrated attention and hair-trigger responses to linguistic register and the social implications of formal structures.

The difference between then and now is very striking. But it is liable to be over-interpreted today. The visual effects of the Elizabethan stage are particularly likely to be discounted because they cannot compare with modern effects. It is only when seen in its own terms that the Elizabethan language of visual effects can be believed to be powerful enough to be an essential part of the greatest body of drama in the modern world, which, whatever we would like to think about it, was in fact a 'seeing' drama and not a reading drama.[2] The problem of arguing this point is in part a problem of vocabulary, for our very words stress the oddity of the past in relation to the norms of the present. Thus we speak of the Elizabethan 'bare' stage. But 'bare' is a purely comparative concept. No one entering the Globe registered, 'Oh I see Master Shakespeare is having one of his bare-stage productions'. Bareness was a norm, not an oddity, and it could only have registered as the absence of any departure from the norm. It was a neutral precondition which allowed other visual effects to make their full impact. The

---

[1] Heywood, *Dramatic Works* (Pearson Reprint edn.), IV (1874), 312.
[2] The general topic has been illuminatingly discussed by I-S. Ewbank, 'More Pregnantly Than Words', *Shakespeare Survey 24* (1971), 13–18, and by Dieter Mehl, 'Visual Imagery in Shakespeare's Plays', *Essays and Studies 1972*, 83–100.

number of these effects was limited; but this means less that the visual language was starved than that each item in it had to carry a disproportionately wide range of significances. The Elizabethan stage uses, by and large, a vocabulary of visually registered movements. It was easy on this stage to register entries or exits from outdoors or indoors (to indoors or outdoors), from heaven or from hell, in concord or in opposition to one another ('at several doors'). To the modern theatre-goer this must seem a starved vocabulary, but such a view, concentrating on what we have gained, conceals what we have lost.

Let us look at the first scene of *Titus Andronicus*.[1] The play begins (like most) by moving the characters around the stage:

> *Enter the Tribunes and Senators aloft; and then enter Saturninus and his followers at one door, and Bassianus and his followers at the other, with drums and trumpets.*

A three-pointed diagram is established before our eyes—four-pointed if we assume that the Tribunes and Senators (traditionally hostile) enter separately. Marcus Andronicus (one of the Tribunes) either enters separately to join the group *above* or comes forward from the group (Q and F differ). In either case he holds up the crown for which the groups below must contest. He tells them that a third candidate, Titus Andronicus, has been elected by those above, and summons those below to dismiss their followers and appear before the Senate on the Capitol. So *They go up into the Senate-house* (by separate doors, one must assume); the main stage is cleared and the people on the upper stage retire out of sight, though the understanding is that the Senate meeting is going on up there, just outside the limits of the visible. A new phrasing of the action on the main stage is now prepared by *A Captain*,[2] who

[1] The stage directions derive from the First Quarto, unless otherwise indicated. Compare with my comments on this scene those of Ann Haaker, 'Non sine causa: The Use of Emblematic Method and Iconology in the Thematic Structure of *Titus Andronicus*', *Research Opportunities in Renaissance Drama*, XIII–XIV (1970–71), 143–68.

[2] I am assuming that the Captain here addresses the theatre audience, who at this point represent the Roman mob. If this assumption is not acceptable we must assume instead that enough Romans remain on stage to provide an audience for the Captain's speech.

heralds a formal processional entry (in reminiscence of a Roman Triumph) by Titus, his sons and his prisoners—nine persons named and at least four attendants (*as many as can be* is the original direction). The next phase of stage movement appears when *A Tomb* is opened (over the stage trap presumably) at line 89,[1] and into this there are two processional exits, one with the 'proudest prisoner of the Goths' and one with the coffins of the dead Andronici. Next the Tribunes, with Saturninus, Bassianus *and others* (presumably the Senators again) re-appear (above), marking the climax of the stage use, with a group of at least sixteen persons occupying two levels of the stage (and a number of named corpses in the space below). The political deliberation that was engaged in at line 63 ff. is now, at line 168, enacted in full sight. The Roman civil authority (above) and the armed factions (below) dispute the crown exposed earlier. There is a minor polarization on the upper stage as well when further faction threatens between the *Patricians* (204) and the Tribunes of the People. But this is soon settled. *A long flourish till they come down*, reads F. The upper and main stages, civil authority and military threat, coalesce and prepare the stage for a new confrontation. Bassianus (defeated in his bid for the purple) and Marcus (defeated in his tribunician proposal) exit with Lavinia. Then, after several scuffles, *Enter aloft the Emperor* [Saturninus] *with Tamora and her two sons and Aaron the Moor*. A new upper/lower polarization is thus created. Military faction is now civil authority and looks down on Titus seen alone on the stage as the leader of 'lawless sons' who 'ruffle in the commonwealth of Rome' (312-3). The pattern of the preceding diagram is now repeated: the 'tomb' is re-opened and the slain son interred. But this time the tomb opens on a stage which is empty of all but the shocked family of mourners. The balance between the political life of the main stage and the supernatural pieties of the tomb has

---

[1] J. C. Adams, 'Shakespeare's Revisions in *Titus Andronicus*', *Shakespeare 400*, ed. J. G. McManaway (1964), 177-90, argues that the tomb requires the use of an inner stage (elsewhere 'the distinctive inner-stage trap'). The argument assumes more than it proves. It seems simpler to suppose that the tomb was represented either by a structure covering the centre-stage trap or by the hole in the stage created by opening the trap. It is clearly the same hole that is used for the 'pit' that Quintus and Martius fall into in Act II.

been lost. This point is reinforced by the next entry: *Enter the Emperor, Tamora and her two sons with the Moor at one door. Enter at the other door Bassianus and Lavinia with others.* The confrontation of the two brothers (now reinforced by their wives) takes one back to the opening of the play; but there is now no *above* to represent the overarching stability of Roman institutions. Personal reconciliations at this level now mark only the space for treachery.

The use of the stage spaces in the first scene of *Titus Andronicus* indicates the basic polarizations of the play. The upper stage denotes (on this occasion) the seat of Roman political power, whether Imperial or Republican. The space beneath the stage locates the metaphysical commitment of the traditional Roman to stern self-sacrifice in the interests of the state, to warrior citizenship based on family piety. The space between these two (the main stage) gives to the principal characters, Titus and Lavinia, who are responsive to both these pressures, a field appropriate to their endeavour throughout the play to bridge the gap between the world of Power and the world of Right. Titus shoots arrows bearing his complaints into the heavens, and seeks to 'pierce the inmost centre of the earth' with descriptions of his wrongs until, in what is both an answer and a mockery of his need for an answer, Tamora appears as Revenge, 'sent from below/To join with him and right his heinous wrongs' (v.ii.3–4). But what begins as cruel mockery ends as cruel justice. After the slaughter of Act V editors usually state that *Lucius, Marcus and their friends go up into the balcony*, so that it is from this significant vantage-point that they deliver their pacificatory speeches to the populace and see Lucius elected Emperor.[1] They only descend, it would seem, when the transfer of power is complete and then the family tomb can be re-opened and the dead Titus and Lavinia interred there. By the end

[1] This editorial stage direction derives from the later offer of Marcus and Lucius to 'headlong hurl' themselves 'from the place where you behold us pleading' (l. 130), and the demand from the floor of the stage to 'come, come . . . and bring our emperor' (ll. 137–8). The latter words clearly state what is implicit throughout the passage, that there is a physical space between the speakers and their audience; the easiest way to secure such a space would be to place them on the balcony. But see J. C. Maxwell's note to v.iii.66 (in his New Arden edition) for a contrary view.

of the play the visual diagram of meaning has been re-stabilized, and the movement of persons to their proper and appointed places assures us that the action is at an end.

As I have noted above, the modern spectator is liable to think this visual language of diagrammatic movement neither very exciting nor very visual. The reason for our disengagement comes in part from our imprisonment in a sense of man's relation to his environment which is characteristically modern. In modern drama characters tend to be 'found' on the stage, absorbed in the activity appropriate to their (painted) environment. Maids are found dusting the furniture, authors writing at their desks, visitors viewing the landscape, hostesses dispensing tea. There is a generalized and unargued modern sense that we are all as we are because our environment made us so; so that an authorial display of physical environment is equivalent to an explanation of character. Thus to display the slum is to explain the criminal; the rich kid has to struggle if he is to evade the legacy of the big house and the retinue of servants. These assumptions and the techniques associated with them are even more obvious in film and television; and Shakespeare on film is no less subject to this modernity than are more modern authors. The Zeffirelli film of *Romeo and Juliet* declined to use dialogue till a camera in a helicopter had surveyed the rooftops of a 'real' Verona. The irregular tiles, the peeling stucco, the narrow streets and open squares, the intense sunlight and the deep shadow—these environmental features are presented to us as explanations of an intense, passionate, intimate and irrational life. To some extent *Romeo and Juliet* is indeed patient of such an explanation; but some parts of it are not. The approach required the savage cuts that followed.

The Elizabethan assumption, if one can judge it from the conduct of their plays, was opposite. Characters are not 'found'; even those who arrive from a 'discovery space' make their presence real by claiming position in that field of force that the open stage represents. It is clear that beds, thrones, desks, etc. were pushed out on to the main stage after their 'discovery' and there claimed their relationship to the world around them. If in modern drama environment is presented as the creator of character, in

Elizabethan drama the character, his entry and his movement create, in so far as we are required to assume one, the environment that is appropriate to his deeds. The actor did this by projecting upon the neutral or generalized diagram of stage space the shape of his fictional life, and the audience then supplied the visual particularities. As Harley Granville Barker says in an interesting early essay:

> ... these things existed *ad hoc* only, and for the actors's convenience. They had, so to speak, no life and no rights of their own ... The true landscape lay in the characters and the tale of themselves that they told.[1]

Thus an actor moves from the main stage to the upper level and says, 'I'll to bed'; we have no difficulty in understanding that he has moved to his bedroom. At a later point the same actor may make the same movement and cry defiance to the besiegers. We easily understand that the upper stage is now the battlements of a city.[2] Indeed in the middle of one scene a character may indicate that he is no longer part of a state occasion but is having a private conversation; if we wish to conceive that he has moved from the audience chamber to the withdrawing room, then our sympathetic response simply makes it so. This is in fact the situation in *Hamlet*, Act I, scene ii. The scene involves a speech from the throne and a dispatch of Privy Council business and so it may be assumed to take place where eighteenth-century editors located it —in 'A Room of State in the Castle'. But at line 128 all the

[1] 'A note upon chapters XX and XXI of *The Elizabethan Stage*', R.E.S. I (1925), 63.

[2] In this sense the simple permanent structure of the Elizabethan stage has an obvious continuity with the 'simultaneous staging' of the later Middle Ages. On that stage the buildings became 'real' (the Nativity stable, the Temple, Herod's palace, Calvary) when the characters occupied them, but the particularity of place fades when the characters no longer focus upon it. With greater flexibility but using the same principles the Elizabethan actors create 'realities' around them, relying on the simple primary qualities of *above, below,* and (no doubt) upstage and downstage. Ben Jonson's *Bartholomew Fair* offers a particularly obvious example of this survival. See Appendix II to the Yale edition of *Bartholomew Fair*, ed. Eugene M. Waith (1963).

characters leave except Hamlet. The first soliloquy *could* be delivered in the room of state, and scenic productions are obliged to make it so. But there is no reason to suppose that it is: Hamlet is not energizing any locale and gives the audience no requirement to imagine a scenic location. Then at line 159 *Enter Horatio, Bernardo, Marcellus*. We are now in a world of friendly and relaxed relationships, somewhere between the formal world of the court and the anguished solitariness of the soliloquy. The place is any place where such relationships can be easily imagined. It becomes, that is, whatever the actions and assumptions of the characters have made it. The shape of the whole scene—from formal entry to solitariness to friendly gathering to exit—is a visual as well as a dramaturgic shape and the patterning, grouping, gathering and dispersal of the characters is what gives structure to its landscape, not the imagination of a set scene. To reinforce this point I may give a second example of the power of actor movement to create visual structures, from the second scene of *Julius Caesar*. The scene begins with an entry in procession of ten named characters *with a great crowd following*. These pass across the stage and after twenty-three lines *Exeunt all but Brutus and Cassius*. The nature of the focus and the quality of the landscape change: we now have a private world to set against the public one preceding, a close-up against a long shot. But against this narrow frontal strip of perception the scene offers tantalizing glimpses of distance. We hear *Flourish and Shout* off-stage. Brutus looks into the distance as it were: 'What means this shouting?' But we are not allowed to see into the distance until at line 177 *Re-enter Caesar with his train*, now set in contrast to the individualized pair, as Brutus comments on Caesar and Caesar makes his remark about Cassius. The stage does not remain so full for long, of course;[1] in a mere thirty lines the procession has swept off again. The pattern re-forms in a new composition of three figures as Casca displays his personal idiosyncrasy (and some essential information). Now, in response to

[1] The economy of the Elizabethan theatre does not seem to allow the stage to be crowded for more than brief and special occasions. The average stage scene (measured across the fifty or so plays I have analysed) has three or four speakers present at one time, though the impression of a crowded public life is often sedulously promoted.

the questions of Brutus and Cassius we are given a verbal picture (from a particular point of view) of the action that was too distant to be seen while Brutus and Cassius were speaking. The stage movement thus sets out a basic diagram of a static foreground of individual life and against that a swirling public movement crossing the line of the other, appearing and disappearing. It is easy to see that this visual component signals much that is essential to an understanding of the play, much that is lost if we cannot visualize the movements of the actors.

Any reader of Shakespeare can supply for himself a list of examples where stage pictures[1] of this kind make a vital contribution to our sense of what is happening in the play. We all respond easily to the rhythm by which groups turn into crowds, break down into twos and threes, form hostile ranks or support a single leader, and we may if we wish imagine scenery appropriate to each grouping. What is less obvious is the difference between this and the modern manner of visual presentation, in which we move from landscapes (largely devoid of individualized figures) to known individuals and then to new landscapes and so to changed persons. In this case it is the procession of landscapes that gives the essential rhythm of the piece, and the individuals have to fit into the interstices of the rhythm so created—desert to city, ghetto to suburb, business district to harbour. In Elizabethan drama the movement from dialogue to soliloquy to dispersed speech to public address integrates the visual and the verbal in a way which serves to conceal the extent to which our understanding depends on visual signals. But the rhythm of movement on to and across the stage is in fact a rhythm of social life into which the words of the characters must be fitted if we are to understand fully what they mean to one another. Radio Shakespeare is a neutered art.

If we allow that the landscape of Shakespeare's stage is a landscape of persons (creating appropriate environments around them),

---

[1] 'Picture' is not an entirely adequate word for what I am referring to. The movements of the actors, as described in the preceding pages, are visual in a simple sense—they are things seen—but they are seldom independently visual; the mind is not allowed to rest merely in the apprehension of what it sees. We have to think of the movements as visual contributions to a totality which depends on the particularities of dialogue to achieve its full reality.

we must also allow that the need to control and integrate this proliferation of environments pushes them into roles as particular kinds of person. A glance through lists of *dramatis personae* for Elizabethan plays will remind us that the persons of these plays tend to be defined by their social status rather than their individual existence. The traditional ordering of the *dramatis personae* by social rank, moving from king to peasant, and with the ladies in a separate *purdah* enclosure at the bottom of the page, is not a gross distortion of the importance attached to rank in the plays them-selves, which are microcosms of life not only as lived but also as organized.[1] Typical inhabitants of the Elizabethan stage world are kings, queens, dukes, counsellors, generals, ambassadors, soldiers, courtiers, clowns, pages, shepherds, watchmen, citizens, sooth-sayers, jailors, friars, Dutchmen, waiting-gentlewomen—charac-ters defined by set role rather than deviant personality.[2] So much is evident; but I suspect that we often misinterpret the evidence by

[1] It is often assumed that this ordering is another part of the general 'tidying-up' or imposition of neo-classical order on Shakespeare's text by eighteenth-century and later editors, the originals being without such lists. It is true that the First Folio has more plays without *dramatis personae* lists than with them. But the authenticity of such listing, and of ordering the characters by rank and by sex, is clear enough from the examples which survive, in seven plays of the First Folio and in innumerable texts of Elizabethan plays of all kinds and dates.

[2] Editors have unthinkingly imposed the prejudices of their time on the material and helped to conceal this aspect of the past. They have resolutely combed texts for the personal names of characters, under the impression that the fullest degree of individualization gives the sharpest meaning to the role. Thus the character called Steward in the original texts of *King Lear* happens to have his personal name—Oswald—mentioned once in the text. Editors seize on this information and convert the regular 'Steward' of the stage directions and speech prefixes into the personal form. They do this with a clear conscience: they believe they are fulfilling Shakespeare's intention. But are they? Almost certainly Shakespeare used the name Oswald because he read in Camden's *Remains* that this was an early English name for a steward. In any case it might be more in keeping with Elizabethan dramaturgy to emphasize Oswald's social status rather than his individuality. His function in the play (like that of Malvolio in *Twelfth Night*) derives from his rank. He is the intimate of gentlemen, but no gentleman; he wears a gold chain, but as a badge of servitude. His loyalty to the vices of his mistress is part of his ambition to rise socially. Compare the character in the same play that the texts generally call Bastard but whom editors call Edmund. Again the social tensions that 'explain' the character arise from the social ambiguity or insecurity of his role.

shining on it the light of our current assumptions. We have a natural tendency to suppose that dukes and friars are the stuff of romance rather than life (we seldom run into them) and that a more realistic treatment would quickly unhusk the 'more real' individual from the 'less real' rank and concentrate our attention on that. There is a recurrent type of modern drama which shows these limiting assumptions in a fairly clear light. This is the kind of play which shows us a set of stereotypical persons, defined by role, caught together in a tense situation. A bank president, a nun, a car-salesman, an interior decorator, a football coach, a student drop-out, are found together trapped in a lift, a hijacked aircraft, an abandoned lifeboat, a jury room. The process that this situation generates is a vivid illustration of the anti-Elizabethan quality of our myths. For though the social roles normally dominate the opening exchanges of these stereotypes and show up their mutual incomprehension and hostility to one another, gradually as the pressure builds up the barriers fall away, leaving exposed the moral that all men (and women) are brothers, and survive because of this. The Elizabethan handling of role and individuality is quite different. Their plays do not move to the discovery that the duke is a man but rather towards a demonstration that the individual is given full meaning only when caught up into his social role, individual characteristics often being explained by social rank— the gracious shepherdess is *really* a princess, the hunchback plotter is not the true king's son, it was the bastard and not the legitimate son that planned the parricide. What is *real* in these terms is less the personal experience and more the social diagram that gives each man his social meaning by relating him to his fellows. At the end of the play the individual returns to his social stereotype because only there can he belong to the validating order.

The closed nature of the social expectation that most Entries give rise to can be seen (I hope) as an essential part of the visual economy that integrates the material of most of these plays, the hierarchic nature of the movements giving us a clear perception of their range of social potential. The entry for the second scene of *Hamlet* (as that appears in the Q1 'theatrical' text and the Q2 text supposed close to Shakespeare's manuscript) describes the arrival on stage of a king, a queen, councillors, ambassadors, the prince,[1] and so offers us both confirmation of social assumption and its deformation in the hierarchical misplacing of 'prince'. But even more important than this point (to which I shall return) is the observation that *all* the characters are understood first in terms of rank and function. Every line these characters speak hereafter will complicate our sense of their being; but all that information will be imprinted not on the blank sheet of our minds but on sheets already headed 'King', 'Prince', 'Councillor', etc. Claudius will turn out to be such-and-such a kind of king, Polonius to be such-and-such a kind of councillor; but it is the first moment of their appearance that gives the substantive form to the functional existence that later knowledge will qualify.

I have been speaking here of the list of the *dramatis personae* and of the wording of the entries as if these were true visual elements. Of course they are nothing of the kind; they are convenient to talk about because they organize visual material but they are separate from it. Thus I have spoken of the stage direction describing the entry of characters in the second scene of *Hamlet*; but no one in a theatre ever sees such a stage direction. The audience sees a number of actors walking on to the stage, in a set and dignified order and taking up conventionalized positions in relation to one another. How then do they know what we know by reading the stage direction—that this is a king, queen, councillor, ambassador, etc? Some of the answer is easy. A king is a man who enters first, wears a crown, sits on a throne, and to whom others do obeisance. A queen is a female version of the same, enters second, wears a smaller crown, sits on a lower throne. But how about 'councillor'? We today have no conception of how a Privy Councillor ought to appear, or what significant gestures should define him. But I would not care to be sure that the Elizabethans had no words in their visual vocabulary to describe such a rank. Today we have little sense of dress as specifically designed to tell us about rank so

[1] The Second Quarto reads *Florish. Enter Claudius, King of Denmarke, Gertrad the Queene, Counsaile: as Polonius, and his Sonne Laertes, Hamlet, Cum Alijs.* (*Counsaile: as* is commonly taken as a misprint for *Counsailores*). The *Ambassadors* appear only in the First Quarto; but as this represents memories of the actual stage performance its witness is important.

that we can orient ourselves in relation to others that we see but do not know, and so make the appropriate gestures in response.[1] The Dumb Shows that punctuate Elizabethan plays seem to tell us, however, that the audience of that time could read a wide range of meanings into a collection of clothes. Ecclesiastical uniforms are particularly useful here and the Pope, Cardinals, Bishops, Monks, Nuns and Friars are among the commonest inhabitants of Dumb Shows. But we find also a number of more difficult secular identifications required of us: 'Midwife' and 'Doctor of Physic',[2] 'Nurse',[3] 'Ambassadors',[4] 'Councillors and Pensioners',[5] 'Roman Senators',[6] 'Senators',[7] 'Mufti' and 'Turks,'[8] 'Master of a ship',[9] 'Herald',[10] 'Maiden of Honour',[11] 'Serjeant, with a mace under his girdle',[12] '[a devil] . . . in black robes like a pronotary',[12] 'Nymphs attired accordingly',[13] 'an Irishman'.[13] All these seem to appear in contexts where recognition of the 'character' must precede understanding of the action. That Elizabethan

---

[1] We may have more than we think. When I was lecturing on this material in 1974 I was given a page from the current 'Instructions to Students' of an American University. This states (*inter alia*) that 'Students are required to wear conventional dress on the campus' and then proceeds to define the convention: . . . the following is regarded as conventional dress:

(a) Suit, collar and tie, shoes and socks, or
(b) Jacket, long trousers, collar and tie, shoes and socks, or
(c) Safari suit of plain-coloured material, of good quality and standard cut, with matching long or short trousers of the same material and colour, shoes and socks, subject to the condition that:
(i) Shoes (definitely not sandals) and matching stockings to be worn with short trousers;
(ii) No article of clothing worn under the jacket should be visible; etc.

[2] Brome, *The Queen and Concubine*
[3] Fletcher, *Four Plays in One*
[4] Fletcher, *The Prophetess*
[5] Dekker, *The Whore of Babylon*
[6] Markham, *Herod and Antipater*
[7] Marston, *Antonio's Revenge*
[8] Daborne, *A Christian Turned Turk*
[9] Heywood, *The Silver Age*
[10] Anon., *Two Noble Ladies*
[11] Wilmot, *Tancred and Gismunda*
[12] Barnes, *The Devil's Charter*
[13] Hughes, *The Misfortunes of Arthur*

audiences were more expert at this kind of recognition than we are is hardly surprising. They after all were still living in the period of sumptuary legislation when there was a statutory garb for every role in society and when dressing outside one's function was still punishable by fines or by placing in the stocks. There can be little doubt that the system was in serious decline by the later years of Elizabeth's reign (and no doubt there was a tense area of age/youth conflict for that reason). But the Act of 24 Henry VIII (1533), cap. xiii, was reaffirmed by Parliament as late as 1597 (as it had been eight times already in the Queen's reign). One paragraph from the Henrician Act may be quoted to show how intertwined were economic and nationalist interests with the desire to maintain hierarchy by keeping lower and higher ranks separable at a glance:

> Serving men and other yeomen taking wages may not wear cloth in their hose above 2s. a yard, nor hose garded or mixed with any other things that may be seen through the upper part of the hose, but with the same cloth only ... nor any furs except grey coney, lamb ... of home growth, nor any foreign bonnet or shirtband; they may wear a silk ribband for their bonnet and their master's badge ... and also they and any other persons may wear on their bonnets all prizes of silver ... won by them in wrestling, leaping, casting the bar, etc.
>
> (XIII, p. 1)

The Act was repealed in the first year of James's reign, but for all that the contrast between the dress of citizens and tradesmen and that appropriate to gentlemen remains a potent factor in the staged conflicts between citizens and gentlemen in the plays of Jonson and Middleton. In *Eastward Ho*, written by Marston, Jonson and Chapman in 1604, just after the repeal, we meet one Francis Quicksilver, an apprentice bound to the London goldsmith, Touchstone, and therefore, technically, a citizen. As an apprentice he has his appropriate statutory garb, coat and flat cap. But as Quicksilver tells us quickly, he has another status: 'tho' I am a prentice I can give arms, and my father's a justice o' peace by descent' (I.i.119–20) and elsewhere: 'my mother's a gentlewoman and my father a justice of peace and of quorum ... although I am a younger brother and a prentice' (I.i.26–9). To keep up with this heritage he wears a fine cloak (only possible to a citizen if he is an alderman, as his master points out) and a sword. He keeps a chest of fine clothes in the house of the usurer Security. All this is clearly contrary to the City Ordinance of 1582[1] which forbade apprentices to wear clothes other than the statutory items given them by their masters or to keep clothes anywhere except in their masters's houses. In Act II we see him in the process of transforming himself into another rank: *Enter Quicksilver in his prentice's coat and cap, his gallant breeches and stockings, gartering himself.* He has broken his indentures and has been turned out of his master's house:

> Bring forth my bravery.
> Now let my trunks shoot forth their silks concealed;
> I now am free, and now will justify
> My trunks and punks. Avaunt, dull flat cap, then!

[1] Printed in Nichols, *The Progresses of Queen Elizabeth* (3 vols. 1788), II. *204–*206: 'Regulations for the Apparel of London Apprentices'. The preamble of the document tells us that 'Luxury having greatly prevailed in this city amongst people of all degrees, but in particular among apprentices, in their apparel etc. which was justly apprehended might prove of dangerous consequence to their masters: for the remedying of which, and preventing the bad effects thereof, 'twas by the common council enacted . . .' Ten sumptuary regulations follow, of which I may give the gist:

1 Only apparel given by the master is to be worn.

2 'To wear no hat within the city and liberty thereof . . . but a woolen cap, without any silk in and about the same . . .'

3 'To wear no ruffles, cuffs, loose collar . . .'

4 'To wear no doublets but what were made of canvas, fustian, sackcloth . . .'

5 Only white, blue or russet hose to be worn.

6 'To wear little breeches . . .'

7 'To wear a plain upper coat of cloth or leather . . .'

8 'To wear no other surtout than a cloth gown or cloak, lined or faced with cloth [only] . . . with a fixed round collar . . .'

9 'To wear no pumps, slippers nor shoes, but of English leather . . .'

10 'To wear no sword, dagger or other weapon but a knife; nor a ring, jewel of gold, nor silver, nor silver nor silk in any part of his apparel'.

For offences against these ordinances the prentice is first to be warned and then whipped, the master who connives at the offences is to be fined. Furthermore (and of further relevance to the case of Francis Quicksilver) it was enacted 'That no apprentice should frequent, or go to any dancing, fencing, or musical schools; nor keep any chest, press, or other place for the keeping of apparel or goods, but in his master's house, under the penalties aforesaid'.

Via, the curtain that shadowed Borgia!
There lie, thou husk of my envassalled state.

(II.ii.34–9)

The change of dress is here the visual expression of a breach with
social reality. As an apprentice Quicksilver was somebody; as a
fake gentleman he is nobody, an outside without an inside, and so
perilously vulnerable to society's revenge on those who defy its
norms, as the play shows. At a later point Quicksilver, the fake
gentleman, and Sir Petronel Flash, the hollow knight ('he who
stole his knighthood on the grand day, for four pounds'), are
shipwrecked in the Thames while trying to escape to Virginia
with their ill-gotten gains. They are apprehended and press-ganged
for the army as 'masterless men', but claiming that they are
gentlemen (and so exempt from the press) are carried before the
magistrate. With sharp irony he counters their claim: 'What? A
knight and his fellow thus accoutred? Where are their hats and
feathers, their rapiers and their cloaks?' (IV.ii.223–5). Those who
have relied on their clothes to establish their gentility, when their
behaviour has been quite ungentle, are properly denied status as
soon as they have lost their clothes. For there are no other criteria
by which they can reclaim what they have lost. The prodigal
apprentice can only restore himself by falling as far below the just
clothing of his rank as he soared above it in the days of his prosper-
ity. At the end of his purgation in prison he is restored to his
master's house. When he was first imprisoned, we are told, 'he gave
away all his rich clothes ... among the prisoners' (V.ii.55–6). He
is left, presumably, in mere rags or shameful undergarments. But
when he is due to return home to his apprenticeship he refuses the
loan of apparel from the jailor, 'but here make it my suit that I
may go home through the streets as a spectacle or rather an
example to the children of Cheapside' (V.v.214–17). The restoration of order at the end of the play is signalled as a return to a
proper sense of clothing, the visual sign of social self-knowledge
and mental balance.

The signalling of changes in socio-moral status through changes
in clothing is nowhere more clearly expressed than in *King Lear*,

particularly in the history of Edgar. The purgatorial process of this play is represented at every level by changes of clothes and by mis-representations of order in the 'speaking pictures' of conventional garments. Lear himself begins as a crowned king and becomes a 'naked wretch'. In the depth of his repudiation of social meaning what he tears off, however, is not simply his physically protective clothing (as we tend to think) but the insignia of his rank, which he had earlier relied on to indicate the continuity of his identity:

Does any here know me? . . . Who is it that can tell me who I am?
(I.iv. 248–52)

The modern reader has a tendency to argue that the stripping of Lear is a movement from false to true: dressed in flowers he is in touch not only with Nature but also with his own deepest nature. But the point is dangerously half-true. The King rejects social order and proclaims his kinship with the animals, not only in words but also in clothing. But he can only do so in isolation and madness; the restoration of peace, concord, relationship is shown by a restoration of socially defining garments put on him in his sleep by the daughter who wishes to honour him and understand him as the social figure she had always known. The social signifi-cance of the garments that Lear wears and takes off is of course only part of the resonance set up by Lear's development. The voyage of Edgar is more obviously social and therefore offers a safer paradigm of the ways in which changes of clothes chart changes of status. He begins as the heir to Gloucester, bearing perhaps the armorial insignia associated with that earldom.[1] Act II, scene iii is the kind of transformation scene we have already noted in the history of Quicksilver in *Eastward Ho*, though it belongs to a more abstracted image of society. Edgar's disguise is to be the nakedness—however that was represented—of the

[1] It seems probable that the stage offered its audiences, daily accustomed to seeing men in livery, some simplified indicators of genealogy and heraldry, attached to the most famous peerages—Gloucester, Warwick, York and Lancaster, Norfolk, Kent, Suffolk. It is worth noticing that the escutcheon of Gloucester would serve for some seventeen surviving plays, that of York for nineteen.

Bedlam beggar. His nakedness is to be social no less than physical: by complete passivity he becomes totally invisible to all the purposes of the plot. The climb back into action and identity is a climb into clothes. The first set is, significantly enough, quite neutral, and its social meaning dependent on the whim of the mad King: the blanket that Lear procures for him is in turn Persian, judicial and Athenian in the mad scenarios that Edgar has to act out. Next he wears the 'best 'parell' that the poor man gives him to guide Gloucester. He is now no longer a Bedlamite (outside society) but a 'most poor man/made tame to fortune's blows'—at the bottom of the heap. Next he is a nameless but socially significant challenger in the armour of a nobleman, though the armour is unmarked. Finally, lifting his beaver I assume, 'My name is Edgar and thy father's son'. It would not be surprising if at this point Edgar picked up the scutcheon of the Gloucesters (which Edmund has been falsely displaying) and made it his own.

The formality of clothing and the precision of the social meanings they can bear allow the dramatists to arrange the visual diagrams on the stage not only in clear demonstration of a closed social situation but also with indications of the instabilities that threaten that order, suggesting also perhaps something of the transformations that may be necessary before the inner pattern of desires and the outer pattern of formal relationships can be brought into a stable alignment. I have already spoken of the malformation of social order in the Q2 Entry for the second scene of *Hamlet*. Hamlet enters, not in the formal position of precedence his rank entitles him to but as a laggard in the rear of the procession. Not only in precedence but also in clothes Hamlet appears as a walking question mark against the rest of the scene. Is the court in mourning for the late king or not? Claudius's speech from the throne tries to have it both ways. He speaks, he says,

> With an [sc. one] auspicious and a drooping eye,
> With mirth in funeral, and with dirge in marriage,
> In equal scale weighing delight and dole.
>
> (I.ii.11–13)

But there can be little doubt that his clothes give the lie to this profession of a balanced attitude. Of course we know from texts like Sidney's *Arcadia* that clothes are sometimes presented as capable of this degree of ambiguity. Thus Amphialus when he approaches the princess he both loves and injures is said to be careful of his clothes's colour:

> lest, if gay, he might seem to glory in his injury and her wrong; if mourning it might strike some evil presage unto her of her fortune. At length he took a garment more rich than glaring, the ground being black velvet richly embroidered with great pearl and precious stones ... but they set so among tuffes of cypress that the cypress was like black clouds through which the stars might yield a dark lustre. About his neck he ware a broad and gorgeous collar [of two parts] ... the one was of diamonds and pearl set with a white enamel ... seemed like a shining ice, the other piece being of rubies and opals had a fiery glistering, which he thought pictured the two passions of fear and desire.
>
> (Arcadia, Book III. *Works*, ed. Feuillerat, I.367)

One can, if one wishes, think of Claudius's clothing as speaking his ambiguity with this degree of elaboration, but it seems improbable that such Arcadian nuances were available to the audience at the Globe. The economy of the scene as well as the economics of the theatre make it likely that the clothes of Claudius, Gertrude and the rest of the court express the 'auspicious' ... 'mirth' ... 'delight' side of the marriage/funeral dilemma. Only Hamlet the laggard has not cast off his nighted colours and stands against the prevailing happiness. He is, however, as we must know, the hero of the play. And therefore we must wonder if the attitude expressed by his movement and his clothes as well as his words is not to be the preferred one, however isolated and cornered. Our visual experience, even alone, can give us something of the basic shape of the conflict in the play. At a later point Hamlet's dress becomes (we are told) even more hectically aberrant and challenging. Ophelia informs us how he came visiting:

> his doublet all unbrac'd,
> No hat upon his head, his stockings fouled,
> Ungart'red, and down-gyved to his ankle.
>
> (II.i.78–80)

There is no reason to doubt her; these are the visual equivalents to the 'wild and whirling words' of his antic disposition. Clothes cannot convey, of course, the complex derangements of sense that Hamlet's actual language gives us. But Ophelia's words amply define the expectation of order against which the aberrant individual makes his mark. 'No hat upon his head' she remarks with appropriate dismay: for the hat was, above all other garments, the essential signal of rank, coming in many significant shapes and sizes, doffed for respect and retained for superiority.[1] Most modern stage Hamlets would sooner appear in a fig-leaf than a hat; but this measures only their distance from the original conditions of the play. In a system so tight, so ordered, so punitive as the Elizabethan social system the smallest shift of priorities made a disproportionately loud signal of rejection or disaffection; and this opened up to the dramatists a method of putting the system and its challengers in immediate visual opposition. Hamlet's hat is an essential part of Hamlet's play.

The opening scene of *Julius Caesar* offers us further examples of the same technique. We meet here a number of Roman citizens enjoying a holiday from trade. In Elizabethan England, holidays and the attire associated with them were regulated by statute.[2] The same is assumed to be true of the Roman workmen. The tribunes scold them:

> Is this a holiday? What! know you not,
> Being mechanical, you ought not walk
> Upon a labouring day without the sign

---

[1] In Act III, scene i of *King Lear* we are told of the mad king that 'unbonneted he runs/and bids what will take all' (ll. 14–15). The king's bonnet is, of course, a protection against the rain, and old gentlemen of eighty shouldn't get wet. But more is involved than this. He is observed to have thrown aside all expression of his ritual dignity, declaring himself by the most obvious visual signal the unprivileged victim of appetite ('And bids what will take all').

[2] Statute of 13 Eliz. (1571), cap. XIX.

Of your profession? Speak, what trade art thou?
First citizen Why, sir, a carpenter.
Marullus Where is thy leather apron and thy rule?
What dost thou with thy best apparel on?

(I.i.2–8)

Once again, as in *Hamlet*, dress is used to mark a questioning of an initial assumption. The costumes imply one thing—a holiday, and so a rejoicing over Caesar's defeat of Pompey. The alternative costume would imply opposite attitudes—a resolute support for Republican government. But which is the right costume? The observation that this is a situation in which 'right' is highly ambiguous takes us close to the centre of this play, and takes us by a route along which the ambiguity of what we *see* is an important signpost.

Several of the particular effects I have spoken about in the course of this essay are associated with disguise. The dependence of the Elizabethan stage on the meanings that clothes give to social groupings, setting out at a glance the structure and potential of what we see, helps to explain the obsession with disguise plots. We ought to consider here the underpinning religious conception of 'labouring in one's vocation',[1] which made the social order (discernible through clothes) part of the will of God. The theory of vocation came very close to making an appropriate set of clothes the precondition of a Christian identity. And inside such preconceptions it can hardly surprise us that Elizabethan dramatic characters regularly take it that any man dressed as a sailor 'is' a sailor. When a husband, wife, father, son, sister returns to the ancestral threshold dressed as a milkmaid, friar or gypsy no one in the house thinks it proper to ask, 'Who *is* this friar, milkmaid, etc?' The question seems central to us because it picks up our primary concern with the individuality behind the role. But the Elizabethan stage was poorly adapted to deal with such questions. Though we in the audience are often invited to attend to the ironies of clashing identities, the characters of the play are normally

[1] See the 'Homily Against Excess of Apparel' in the *Sermons or Homilies Appointed to be Read in Churches in the Time of Queen Elizabeth* (rept. 1817).

imprisoned inside the assumption that things are as they seem, the new man in a blue coat to be judged as a good servant or a bad servant but not as anything wantonly different. It is the skill of the actor to remind us that the new Caius is the old Kent; but the writing seems designed to make him procure this effect by brittle virtuosity rather than 'character study'. His roles remain effectively separate from one another as he shuffles one behind the other in the manner of a card-sharper; he is not invited to draw them together as facets of a single unifying personality, but to point outwards to the different social worlds he has inhabited. Our knowledge of unity is continually played against the theatrical evidence of diversity.

It has long been evident that Elizabethan theatrical effects, like modern operatic effects, work through separate high moments rather than by slow accumulative pressure. Critics of the school of Shücking and Stoll long ago noted this point, but took it to be evidence of a 'primitiveness' of technique. Outside a rigidly pro-gressivistic view of history this does not seem a very useful vocabulary. But the fact of difference does remain and powerfully affects our sense of what an actor can do with a Shakespearian role, particularly when that role involves disguise. The expectation of rigidity and so clarity of expression in social relationships meant that the Elizabethan audience brought to the theatre an anticipa-tion of typed social behaviour that the actor could easily refer to and exploit. The servant's cringe, the soldier's swagger, the grandee's frown, the fop's simper, and the whole vocabulary of social deference and authority, gave the actor a repertory of faces and gestures on which he could practise his virtuosity and enliven his audience. This is certainly how Richard Robinson, celebrated as an actor of female parts, is seen in Ben Jonson's *The Devil is an Ass*. One character describes to another how Robinson (in a real life situation) acted the part of a lawyer's wife:

> But to see him behave it
> And lay the law, and carve and drink unto them,
> And talk bawdy and send frolics! Oh,
> It would have burst your buttons and not left you
> A seam.
>
> (II.viii.71–5)

Indeed it is Robinson's praise not only to be like a real woman, but to appear more womanly than most women (lines 76–7), for his performance is concentrated by art, not dissipated in the varieties of nature.

The modern actor, at least in the West—for the *onnagata* playing female roles in the Kabuki theatre excites much the same technical interest in virtuosity as did Richard Robinson—is expected to feel himself into a role as if the traits of the character were his own, supplying a unifying history for that kind of person (from the so-called 'sub-text') and projecting himself into the auditorium as a real Othello, Morose or Flamineo. And the modern audience often makes sense of the play by using its recognition of the actor or actress as clues to the nature of the person being played. The 'star' system builds on this. 'That's Gielgud and that's Brando' we say to ourselves, watching the Hollywood version of *Julius Caesar*, as we try to bring the character as close as possible to the supposed personality of the actor. Sometimes, indeed, as in the last scene of John Barton's production of *Richard II* (Stratford-upon-Avon, 1973), it is essential for the spectators to recognize the actors if they are to understand what the director is doing to the play.[1] There is little or no impulse in such a mode of acting to play up the clash between the physical attributes of the actor and the nature of the role he is playing. But such a clash is an essential part of any theatre in which males play female roles.[2]

This aesthetic of clash is not the most obvious feature of Shakespeare's *travesti* roles, but it is an essential element all the same. The praise of the boys playing these parts must always have been praise for a role *used* rather than a role *achieved*. Portia does

[1] See Stanley Wells, *Furman Studies* (June, 1976), 79–80.

[2] The last refuge of this aesthetic is in the performances of male and female impersonators (the former almost extinct). Among female impersonators the burlier the actor the more startling his success at feminine walking, etc. Danny La Rue's frequent reference to his (male) genitalia serve the same function: they 'alienate' the audience and remind us to enjoy the skill of the illusion *as illusionism*. See Jack Waterman in *The Listener* for 8 February 1971: Danny La Rue, he says, 'is able to radiate an extraordinary allure as well as send up the whole idea of glamour ... we have this apparently glamorous creature who, from the first 'Wotcher mates', instantly defuses the disbelief that it is a man' (218).

not disappear into Balthazar, nor Rosalind into Ganymede, but makes us conscious of the actor's capacity to invent new character-istics to answer new responsibilities, weakening our sense of a central core of character in order to strengthen our wonder at the co-existence of the separate effects. With typical Shakespearian evasiveness (alias magnanimity) these plays do not forbid us to imagine unified personalities to which all the separate displayed characteristics belong; but they frequently challenge the critic with genuine problems.

The problems cannot be evaded, and indeed are overwhelming, in several non-Shakespearian plays of the period, which probably give us a more accurate sense of what disguise and *travesti* roles offered to the average Elizabethan theatre-goer. George Chap-man's *The Blind Beggar of Alexandria, most pleasantly discoursing his variable humours in disguised shapes full of conceit and pleasure* (1596) tells the story of Irus, the blind beggar of the title, who also passes in the city as Leon, a wealthy usurer (with the aid of a large nose), as Count Hermes and as Duke Cleanthes. The interest of the play does not arise from our response to the 'real' man who plays all these roles; who he is remains unknown until the last scene and even then remains obscure. The interest arises rather from the breakneck speed of change and the danger of discovery, the rapid movement of intrigue that is fuelled by disguise. The impulse behind the play is that of the conjurer—to put more and more balls into the air, yet to avoid the danger of always imminent collapse. Thus, as Hermes, the protagonist marries one lady, then, as Leon, he marries another. But this is not enough. He then cuckolds himself twice, seducing Hermes's wife as Leon and Leon's wife as Hermes. Finally as Cleanthes he marries off the doubly deceived ladies to some spare kings in his entourage. The anonymous his-tory play, *Look About You* (1600) offers an even more dizzying progress. Much of the play consists of a frenetic chase in which Skink, a murderer supposed hermit, steals the clothes of Redcap the jailor's son, and is then forced to give up Redcap's clothes to Gloster (also on the run). Dressed as Gloster, Skink then success-ively steals the clothes of Prince John, Geoffrey the barman, a hermit-conjurer, a falconer, and then a hermit again. In parallel incidents Gloster (as Redcap) appears in his turn as Old Faulconbridge, as a pursuivant and as a hermit. Meanwhile Lady Faulconbridge has become 'a merchant's wife' while Robin Hood (in minority) dresses as Lady Faulconbridge. The overall effect is that of a game of hide-and-seek in which the danger of discovery is always avoided at the last possible moment, when a new suit of clothes and so a new range of social exploitation becomes available. The motivating purpose of such plays is survival; and so it is, in a more buried way, in *Twelfth Night* and *As You Like It*. But Shakespeare's slower and more ruminative plotting can avoid the pressures of a set social situation more easily than the faster moving plots of *Look About You* or *The Blind Beggar of Alexandria*. In these plays social stereotypes are a necessity if we are to recognize quickly enough the staging posts of the plot as the intrigue flashes past them. Thus the disguise roles in *Look About You* consist of previously identified characters, usually with a strong bias to the type (Old Faulconbridge as the jealous dotard, John the malcontent prince), and of social types, wearing a recognized uniform (pursuivant, hermit, falconer, herald, serving-man, barman). The range of behaviour we can expect is thus appropriately reduced. The one exception is Redcap, the jailor's son; and I take it that his name (and the object it signifies) is devised to be sufficient identification for one without social function. At a less extreme level of complexity, but offering the same suggestion that disguise operates most sharply when the role chosen is signalled by uniform as one having clearly prescribed duties and a restricted range of behaviour, are the *lazzi* of the trickster Cockledemoy in Marston's *The Dutch Courtesan* (1605) who becomes in turn a barber, a French pedlar, a bellman, a serjeant (or arresting officer).

The skill of the actor whose profession not only required him to appear in quick-change disguises but regularly to double wildly dissimilar roles[1] one after the other responds to a general taste of

[1] Thus from the 'plot' of Peele's *The Battle of Alcazar* (as performed somewhere between 1597 and 1602) we learn that Samuel Rowley played (1) a Moorish Attendant, (2) Pisano (a captain), (3) a Messenger, (4) a Moorish Ambassador, (5) a Devil, (6) a Captain of Tangier, (7) Death, (8) a Portuguese soldier, while Robert Shaa played an Irish Bishop, the Governor of Tangier, and Celebyn (a Moorish nobleman). In *The Fair Maid of the Exchange* (pub-

the time for acting as acting rather than as character portrayal. In terms of the visual dimension of the stage this taste shows itself in the frequency with which the individual is asked not only to belong to a set social scene (shown by dress, movement, etc.) but also to subvert the expectation that the audience has erected on these bases. The function of the disguised or undisguised subverter is in these terms rather like that of the so-called 'false relationship' in music, where a dominating harmonic connexion is temporarily contradicted by a passing relationship, and where, in the more complex examples, the contradiction can resolve either way. So the contradiction between Hamlet and the court of Claudius resolves in favour of the dissonant prince rather than the consonant king. But no new consonance is set up thereby, for Hamlet remains too obliquely related to any consensus for a new harmonic system to form around him. The popularity of characters who both belong and do not belong to the dominant social harmony is another indicator of the same taste—stewards (who are both gentlemen and non-gentlemen), bastard noblemen, disguised rulers, counterfeit captains, feigned madmen. All these operate to keep the pattern open and to prevent the set social expectations that the scene conveys to our eyes from seeming to tell the whole truth.

The role of Vindice in *The Revenger's Tragedy* offers a different model of the interrelationship between the disguising individual and the fixed world around him. Tourneur (if he is the author) is like Shakespeare in his willingness to allow that the different roles of the hero are unified inside a single personality. Indeed the play is built up on the assumption that Vindice is the visible manipulator of his own performances; but it also shows that his character is disintegrated by this fact. Vindice's 'honest' brother, Hippolyto, is asked to supply a pandar for the duke's son. He introduces Vindice as Piato ('Mr Hidden'). The disguise is presented as more than a physical change:

---

lished 1607) one actor plays Scarlet (a highwayman), Flower ('a humorous old man'), Master William Bennet (a young gentleman) and an Arresting Officer. In *Mucedorus* (published 1598) one actor plays Comedy, a Boy, an Old Woman and Ariena.

Vindice   What, brother? am I far enough from myself?
Hippolyto   As if another man had been sent whole
  Into the world, and none wist how he came.
Vindice   It will confirm me bold, the child o' th' court.
  Let blushes dwell i'th' country.

(I.iii. 1–5)

Vindice believes himself to be in charge of the change, simply
adapting to new circumstances. But the language points to what
the play will eventually prove, that the new born 'child o' th'
court' is a separate creation that will eventually destroy its
creator. The presence of Piato is not presented simply as an
addition to the stage picture. The pandar's clothes (and presumably the carriage of body that goes with them) releases and confirms a quality of Vindice that could not otherwise appear. His
plot role—to destroy the corrupt court—involves a great deal of
what one would think of as 'playing against the grain'; but just
what the 'grain' is becomes increasingly obscure. When Piato has
served his turn and the duke's son wishes to have him rubbed out
he turns to Hippolyto again, who now introduces Vindice as himself, or as a near version of himself, a discontented country gentleman, Hippolyto's brother. The return to the self has here no
flavour of triumph. Vindice's 'true' face turns out to function in
much the same way as his false face. His 'killing' of Piato is not a
release but another phase in the developing disintegration of self,
judged at the end of the play to be a complete moral collapse.

The morality of *The Revenger's Tragedy* draws on a deeply in-
grained moral suspicion about acting which we may presume the
playwrights knew very well even if they did not share it. If the
call of God is for each man to labour in his own clothes and his
own community in the vocation to which he was born, then the
actor is essentially what the Greek origins of his profession
suggests—a hypocrite (ὑποκριτής = actor). In these terms the
Elizabethan audience's enjoyment of acting as a virtuoso playing
against the set shapes of the social diagram represents a kind of
moral holiday, a catharsis in which actors carry away the wicked-
ness of the audience's fantasies about freedom from vocation. By

making up his character as he went along the actor placed himself outside the moral pale. His work is, not simply in its accidents but in its essence, an implicit attack on the hunger for commonalty and continuity from birth through death that the state and the preachers insisted on. The progress of *The Revenger's Tragedy*, as I have described it, draws on this attitude to equate the power of the actor not only with the fantasy of individual achievement but with the spiritual disintegration that was said to be its concomitant. This moral outlook, towards which the structure of the society and the nature of the profession exerted a powerful pressure, appears again and again in the plays of Shakespeare and his contemporaries. The two longest roles in the Shakespeare canon—Hamlet and Richard III—are also the most actorish. The power and attraction of these famous parts seem to derive less from depth of psychology than from range of potential effects. Few would deny that this is true of Richard III. Without any change of clothes Richard moves from role to role, a loyal brother to Clarence, a love-struck wooer to Lady Anne, a moralist to Hastings, a pious *dévot* to the Lord Mayor, reacting to each new challenge with a new set of faces and an awareness of a new space to be exploited. Richard, like Vindice, embodies the impious fantasy of the individual's unlimited capacity to reshape his world. And the moral cost of his armoury of faces is even more clear. The man of many parts is a man without a centre. In Act V, when the victims of all the games he has played come back to haunt him, he cannot find the self to which the whole of his experience should add up:

> I am a villain; yet I lie, I am not.
> Fool, of thyself speak well. Fool, do not flatter.
>
> (v.iii.190–91)

The 'I' who speaks the lines has lost assurance of the 'me' to whom they refer, for the acts he has staged to trap the others have finally excluded the self.

The action of *Hamlet* cannot be expressed in such a clear moral formula as will serve for *Richard III*. At no point in *Hamlet* is there an explicit moral judgment of the kind noted above for *Richard III*. This cannot excuse us from noting, however, that Hamlet, to survive in a situation in which he is presented as the victim and not the victimizer, has to employ powers of acting very similar to those of Richard and carrying at least some of the same moral taint. It is a large measure of his power and his charm that he can achieve so many effective performances. As mourner, malcontent, madman, lover, statesman, solicitous son, blunt friend, stern moralist, courteous gentleman, critic, he is continuously taking up roles that set him at a tangent to the main action of the play, and so prevent him from being absorbed into consensus attitudes. But the means that detach him from corruption need not themselves be incorrupt. Many of his attitudes (even the condemnation of his mother in the 'closet scene', III.iv) seem as much exercises in the appropriate rhetoric as simple expressions of personality or basic feeling. Hamlet's delight in playing cannot be explained entirely by the need to 'play it safe', to protect himself against Claudius. Thus when he returns from voyaging in Act V and hears Laertes's exclamations against Ophelia's fate he seems to be driven to reveal himself and compete in passion at least as much by the need to show a superior performance as by anything more 'personal'. Again, when the ghost has given his vital information in Act I, scene v we may look to Hamlet for some deeply felt expression of what this story of his father's murder means to him. There are few readers or spectators who have not felt some stab of disappointment, however momentary, that his reaction is so much like a programme for behaviour and so little like a personal response:

> O villain, villain, smiling damned villain!
> My tables—meet it is I set it down
> That one may smile, and smile, and be a villain;
> At least I am sure it may be so in Denmark.
>
> *Writing*
>
> So, uncle, there you are. Now to my word:
> It is 'Adieu, adieu! Remember me'.
> I have sworn't.
>
> (I.v.106–12)

Having fixed these bases of his behaviour he then proceeds to 'act it up' for Horatio and the others, in something like a pilot project for the antic disposition. The means of expressing his attitude are so complex that there is a danger that we will cease to believe in the unifying impulse behind them. We can hardly expect Shakespeare, however, to flee from the danger. The chance to portray a hero who can be all things to all men is one that a competent dramatist can hardly turn down, and the reward of pursuing it is the most famous and most successful play of the modern world. But there is a disadvantage, and it shows itself in the perennial Hamlet-question. The classic approach to *Hamlet* assumes that the complexity of his behaviour is to be referred to a supposed complex personality which underlies it and explains it. But this referral has produced only critical chaos, for there is no agreement on what kind of man Hamlet is or how his actions add up in a unified perception. The commonplace attitudes to acting and the examples of *Richard III* and *The Revenger's Tragedy* suggest that Shakespeare may have been more aware than his modern interpreters of the implications of the doctrine that acting runs counter to vocation where vocation is the guarantor of integrity. But we cannot reduce the play to a simple moral diagram of this kind. Richard III's virtuosity as an actor arises from a clearly defined moral emptiness of self, and the structure of that play leads to a natural judgment: the dull Richmond, who cannot pretend, inherits the kingdom. But Hamlet's play does not develop towards the condemnation of Hamlet the man. His subversions of the set social order are presented sympathetically. Yet the actor's power to undercut expectation, to expose the hypocrisies of others, is not the true power of a prince. Fortinbras would seem to be as much a non-actor as Richmond; but the succession of this simple-minded man does not arise here as the inevitable consequence of the chaos of meaning that the clever and amoral actor has imposed on his society. His final epitaph on Hamlet is ambiguous in the extreme:

> Bear Hamlet like a soldier to the stage.
> For he was likely, had he been put on

> To have prov'd most royal; and for his passage
> The soldier's music and the rite of war
> Speak loudly for him.
>
> (v.ii.388–92)

An absorption of the dead person into the value-system of his encomiast and a 'placing' ritual give Hamlet a final stability that his life showed no signs of developing. His quicksilver mind and quick-darting wit forced us to love him; but the play cannot end without asserting values that the hero signally failed to embody. Are we to take it that our admiration for the hero requires us to assent to this fixing of his image, assuming a posthumous recovery from the improprieties of an acting career? Or are we meant to accept, with anger or resignation, the fact that society defeats the individual? The actual play would seem to be more ambiguous than either of these formulae. By setting up a situation in which acting is the last available resource of the hard-pressed individual Shakespeare is able to express a tension between private life and the status quo which we all recognize as a natural part of our experience. *We* do not know how to resolve the tension and therefore go along happily with the author's evocation of the gap between the individual and society, even though the problem is, as in real life, unresolvable.

In *Hamlet* Shakespeare seems to have done more than take a successful formula and treat it with unexampled richness. He has picked up and embodied much of the essential nature of staging or acting, particularly in the terms of his own day, but also partly in the terms of ours. The visual dimension of the Elizabethan stage suggests a rigid world in which the participating individual is defined by his social role. The plot of the play has a natural tendency to endorse this rigidity, the final values of its movement arising from the restoration of social hierarchy. But the creativity of the individual actor consists precisely in his suspect capacity to move in and out of clothes and postures and so retain freedom of identity in spite of the pressures all around him. The actors both endorse and deny what the plot and the stage says they are and must be: they endorse by fulfilling these expectations; but they deny by modes of fulfilment that they seem to choose for themselves and by assumptions that they are free to do anything else they fancy. Shakespeare continually offers us characters who are so placed that they are impossible to confine. Thus Richard II (no less than Richard III) is a player-king as well as a real king, Falstaff is both a coward and a comedian deliberately playing at being a coward, Cleopatra both a queen and a roguish boy playing at queenliness. The actor reminds us that behind the clothes and the role there remains an unexhausted capacity for new inventions. Shakespearian parts encourage the actor to remain in touch with this ambiguity or 'third dimension' and to continue to give us his sense of freedom, even though the inexorables are closing in around him. As he speaks we hear the accent of free creativity at the same time as the stage shows us the shape of the prison-house.

Marston's 'Antonio' Plays and Shakespeare's 'Troilus and Cressida': The Birth of a Radical Drama

JONATHAN DOLLIMORE

MARSTON'S *Antonio* plays show how individuals become alienated from their society. Bereaved, dispossessed, and in peril of their lives, they suffer extreme disorientation and are pushed to the very edge of mental collapse. The two related senses in which they achieve re-integration—that is, reintegration of self and of self with society—involve the creation of a sub-culture dedicated to revenge: 'vengeance absolute' (*Antonio's Revenge*, III.ii.75).[1]

Running through Marston's dramatization of this process are attitudes to human identity, to revenge and to providence which are radical—radical in the sense of being 'marked by a considerable departure from the usual or traditional':[2] thus, his protagonists are not defined by some spiritual or quasi-metaphysical essence, nor, even, a resilient human essence; rather, their identities are shown to be precariously dependent upon the social reality which confronts them. Correspondingly, revenge action is not a working out of divine vengeance,[3] but a strategy of survival resorted to by alienated and dispossessed individuals. Moreover, in that action is a rejection of the providential scheme which divine vengeance conventionally presupposed.

---

[1] All references to *Antonio and Mellida* and *Antonio's Revenge* are from G. K. Hunter's editions in the Regents Renaissance Drama Series (London, 1965 and 1966).

[2] *Webster's Third New International Dictionary of the English Language* (London, 1961), 1872.

[3] To see it as such is still the orthodox view: 'divine vengeance forms the narrative and thematic center of *each* revenge play' [my italics], R. Broude, 'Revenge and Revenge Tragedy in Renaissance England', *Renaissance Quarterly*, XXVIII (1975), No. 1, 55.

Antonio's Revenge is radical in yet another respect: it eschews the kind of structure which falsifies conflict by *formally* resolving it; instead, the play's structure incorporates and intensifies the sense of social and metaphysical dislocation which is its subject.

In what follows I propose to substantiate this reading of Marston, primarily with reference to *Antonio's Revenge* (*c.* 1600–1), and then explore the extent to which *Troilus and Cressida* (*c.* 1601–2) shares these radical attitudes to identity, revenge and providence, and articulates them through a similar dramatic structure. If my analysis is correct, these two plays, despite their obvious and considerable differences, have thematic concerns and structural characteristics which are not only similar, but seminal for the development of Jacobean tragedy.

I

Antonio and Mellida begins with a battle between two dukes, Piero and Andrugio. Piero wins and Andrugio, together with his son Antonio, is banished. The experience of father and son is one of extreme alienation. They are estranged from family and society, stripped of their former identities, cast out and hunted under sentence of death. Initially they are separated, each believing the other to be dead; Andrugio laments the loss of 'country, house, crown, son' (IV.i.89).

Through the burlesque of Tamburlaine in the Introduction a significant point is being made; Alberto tells Piero to

> ... frame your exterior shape
> To haughty form of elate majesty
> *As if* you held the palsy-shaking head
> Of reeling chance under your fortune's belt
> In strictest vassalage;
>
> (7–11, my italics)

So, Tamburlaine's capacity to 'hold the Fates bound fast in iron chains,/And with my hand turn Fortune's wheel about'[1] is seen as

---

[1] *Tamburlaine*, ed. J. W. Harper (London, 1971), part 1, I. ii. 174–5.

exhilarating fiction, evoking legends of 'Hercules/Or burly Atlas' (18–19) but without the capacity to deceive: 'Who cannot be proud, stroke up the hair and strut?' (14). Such is the fictional aspiration of man but, for Andrugio and Antonio, the reality is different—they, like the 'breast' in the Prologue to *Antonio's Revenge* are impotently 'Nail'd to the earth with grief .../ Pierc'd through with anguish' (22–3). Being nailed to the earth with grief is inextricably bound up with the despairing knowledge of 'what men were, and are,/ ... what men must be' (18–19).[1] I shall come back to *Antonio's Revenge* after further consideration of *Antonio and Mellida*, since the central themes of the former play are anticipated in the latter.

Alienation and grief generate a confusion which is so intense that it threatens Antonio's sanity and brings his very identity into question. In a delirious soliloquy he tells himself: 'Antonio's lost;/ He cannot find himself, not seize himself' (IV.i.2–3; cf. IV.i.102–5). Andrugio's way of responding to all this is to attempt a posture of stoical independence and self-sufficiency (*apathia*):

> ... There's nothing left
> Unto Andrugio, but Andrugio;
> And that nor mischief, force, distress, nor hell can take.
> Fortune my fortunes, not my mind shall shake.
>
> (III.i.59–62)

In this play stoicism is an attempt to redefine oneself solely from within, to reconstitute one's sense of self by withdrawing from the external social reality which has threatened it. As such it is a position precariously attained and incapable of being maintained; attitudes of stoical resistance break down and the stoic becomes 'vile passion's slave' (IV.i.69). The characters of this play attempt to disengage themselves from hostile circumstance but cannot; like Webster later, Marston wanted to show how individuals internalize the confusions and contradictions of their world,

---

[1] Compare Montaigne, who says that man is 'fast tied and nailed to the worst, most senselesse, and drooping part of the world ...', *Montaigne's Essays*, trans. John Florio, Everyman's Library, 3 vols. (London, 1965), II, 142.

becoming themselves confused and contradictory. Faced with a dislocated world, the individual consciousness becomes itself dislocated.

The serious dramatic and philosophical intention I am attributing to Marston is entirely compatible with his attraction to parody and melodrama; they are, in fact, integral to his dramatic vision. Parody was a complex dramatic process for the Elizabethans, not merely a source of comic effect. By the time of the appearance of these plays stoical endurance had been memorably embodied in such figures as Kyd's Hieronmio and Shakespeare's Titus. A philosophical attitude had become a stage convention. Marston, through parody, undermines the convention and, therefore, discredits the attitude. First, there is the self-conscious, sardonic distrust of stage convention as an adequate representation of the experience and the reality which it claims to represent (see especially iv.ii.69–76—discussed below); second, there is distrust of the sufficiency of stoicism as a philosophy of mind; *de contemptu mundi* and stoic *apathia* are no longer viable responses: man may want to be independent of the world but he cannot be; like it or not he is inextricably 'nailed' to it.

This theme is epitomized in the instability and ambivalence of Feliche. In Act III we see him scorning Castilio's social vanity from a position of stoical superiority (iii.ii.41ff.). Within moments his resolve shatters under the pressure of his own egoism and jealousy: 'Confusion seize me .../ Why should I not be sought to then as well?' Andrugio, under the pressure of different but equally contradictory experiences, undergoes a similar collapse (iv.i.46–70).

II

In *Antonio's Revenge* the probing of stoicism, as both attitude and convention, is more searching. In the opening scenes we learn that Andrugio and Feliche have been murdered. It now falls to Pandulpho, Feliche's father, to take up the role of stoic hero. Again, stoicism is in opposition to 'passion'. Pandulpho begins by rejecting the latter, together with its typically hyperbolic mode of expression:

> Would'st have me cry, run raving up and down
> For my son's loss? Would'st have me turn rank mad,
> Or wring my face with mimic action,
> Stamp, curse, weep, rage, and then my bosom strike?
> Away, 'tis apish action, player-like.
>
> (I.ii.312–16)

Notably, it is the theatrical convention, as well as the experience, which is being repudiated: passion is a kind of dramatic posturing.

Pandulpho's stoic resolve lays claim to a perfect transcendence of the event, an ethical resolution of suffering which is beyond the event:

> If he [Feliche] is guiltless, why should tears be spent?
> Thrice blessed soul that dieth innocent.
>
> The gripe of chance is weak to wring a tear
> From him that knows what fortitude should bear.
>
> (I.ii.317–18; 321–2)

When we next encounter Pandulpho his stoicism is even stronger. Piero attempts to corrupt him but cannot and so, in fury, banishes him instead:

> *Piero*   Tread not in court! All that thou hast I seize.
> [*Aside*]   His quiet's firmer than I can disease.
> *Pandulpho*   Loose fortune's rags are lost; my own's my own.
>
> 'Tis true, Piero; thy vex'd heart shall see
> Thou hast but tripp'd my slave, not conquer'd me.
>
> (II.i.166–8; 171–2)

'Slave' according to Hunter is 'the merely physical and temporal aspects of Pandulpho'; so, the basis of his stoicism is transcendence of the temporal, and its corollary, a duality of mind and body: 'The earth's my body's, and the heaven's my soul's/Most native place of birth' (II.i.158–9). Thereafter Pandulpho disappears until Act IV, scene ii where he again preaches fortitude to Antonio. In short, his command of self in the face of the 'grief' and 'anguish' which the Prologue described, appears total.

Suddenly the resolve breaks; his philosophy of noble transcendence is rejected outright:

> Pandulpho Man will break out, despite philosophy.
>   Why, all this while I ha' but play'd a part,
>   Like to some boy that acts a tragedy,
>   Speaks burly words and raves out passion;
>   But when he thinks upon his infant weakness,
>   He droops his eye. I spake more than a god,
>   Yet am less than a man.
>
> (IV.ii.69–75)

What is being rejected here is the Christian-stoic view of man as capable of defining himself from within, independently of the world in which he lives and which acts upon him. Try as he might, Pandulpho was unable to find the spiritual essence which would sustain him in the face of grief and, ultimately, enable him to transcend it altogether. He acknowledges the soul to be earthbound after all: 'I am the miserablest *soul* that *breathes*' (IV.ii.76, my italics). Earlier Pandulpho had repudiated passion as 'mimic action', favouring instead the calm of stoic resolve. Now stoicism is rejected with stage metaphors ('I ha' but play'd a part').

Antonio's attitude to suffering is very different; he wants to confront rather than withdraw (stoically) from it, to be revenged on the world rather than passively endure it:

> Confusion to all comfort! I defy it.
> Comfort's a parasite, a flatt'ring Jack,
> And melts resolv'd despair.
>
> (I.ii.284–6)

At II.ii.47ff. he reads from, only to reject, Seneca's *De Providentia* (VI,6). It is, he says, a philosophy inadequate to the reality of his experience. Antonio has known all along that there is no inner self into which one can withdraw; disorientation penetrates the whole self simply because 'grief's invisible/And lurks in secret angles of the heart' (II.ii.71–2). He endures this grief by translating it into action, into an active search for reintegration. And by IV.ii he realizes that the only avenue to that reintegration is through the role of revenger.

The moment when Pandulpho's resolve suddenly breaks is central for understanding attitudes to identity and the psychology of revenge in Jacobean tragedy. Let me recapitulate what has led to this moment: Marston first of all dramatizes the way that dislocation in the world generates dislocation in consciousness. 'Grief' and all that it stands for in terms of estrangement, alienation, and disorientation threatens not just the individual's capacity to survive in the world, *but his very identity within it*. Pandulpho's stoic strategy proved unsuccessful as a way of coping with this and so he turns to revenge: it enables him to regain his identity, to resist mental collapse, through a purposeful—albeit violent—re-engagement with the world. Antonio speaks for Pandulpho and a generation of revengers when he translates his misery into revenge; he is, he says, 'The wrack of splitted fortune, the very ooze, /The quicksand that devours all misery'. But, he adds,

> For all this, I dare live, and I will live,
> Only to numb some others' cursed blood
> With the dead palsy of like misery.
>
> (IV.ii.18–20)

Suddenly we understand his attitude of 'resolv'd despair' (I.ii.286);

> We must be stiff and steady in *resolve*.
>
> (IV.ii.109, my italics)

> *Resolved hearts* ... Steel your thoughts, sharp your *resolve*, embolden your spirit ...
>
> (V.ii.79–81, my italics)

In *Antonio and Mellida* reintegration, of self and of the self with society, is achieved artificially through the play's tragi-comic denouement; the main characters confer familial identity upon each other (v.ii.225–9) and, after being further consolidated by 'wedlock' (255), their harmony is complete: 'Now there remains no discord that can sound/Harsh accents to the ear of our accord' (251–2). By contrast, in *Antonio's Revenge* reintegration is achieved through the resolve which derives from vengeful commitment. It is as if, in Antonio's words, they have shaken off the 'dead palsy' (IV.ii.20) which afflicts them and undergone a terrible rebirth. They create a new intimacy among themselves, an intimacy which becomes the basis of a ritualistically confirmed counter-culture:

> Let's thus our hands, our hearts, our arms involve.
> *They wreathe their arms.*
>
> (IV.ii.110)

> *Antonio* [to Pandulpho]   Give me thy hand, and thine, most
>   noble heart;
> Thus will we live and, but thus, never part.
> *Exeunt twin'd together.*
>
> (v.ii.88–9)

In this way the disintegrating effects of 'grief' are finally overcome.

Central to the theatre of Bertolt Brecht is a rejection of the notion that nature is unalterable and eternally fixed. Brecht associates this conception of man with what he calls bourgeois or 'Aristotelian' theatre; it erroneously assumed

> ... that people are what they are, and will remain so whatever it costs society or themselves: 'indestructibly human'.[1]

It further assumed that the eternally human, precisely because it is eternal, can be understood independently of man's environment (Willett, pp. 96–7). In challenging these assumptions Brecht is, of course, following the classic Marxist view that human consciousness is determined by social being rather than the converse (Willett, p. 250). Brecht has said of Baal, the nihilistic, anti-social

---

[1] *Brecht on Theatre: the Development of an Aesthetic*, trans. John Willett (London, 1964), 235

'hero' of the play of that name: 'he is anti-social [*asozial*], but in an anti-social society'.[1] There is, I think, an interesting comparison to be made between the revenger-malcontent-satirist figure of Jacobean drama and the protagonists of Brecht's early works. Brecht was, of course, much influenced by Elizabethan-Jacobean drama and not surprisingly since it anticipates his own theatre in important respects. Thus, Marston, like Brecht, shows how the individual's identity, as well as his survival, is dependent upon his relationship to social reality; how alienation dislocates consciousness, and how the individual regains his identity by purposefully re-engaging with society—albeit through brutal behaviour.

III

For Pandulpho, the rejection of a stoic definition of man is inseparable from his rejection of the stoic's conception of providence and natural law:

> . . . all the strings of nature's symphony
> Are crack'd and jar . . .
> . . . there's no music in the breast of man . . .
>
> (iv.ii.92–4)

G. D. Aggeler has argued that in the speech from which these lines are taken,

> Pandulpho is rejecting a belief that underlies all of stoic moral doctrine, the belief in the rationality of Nature. According to the stoics, God imparted a rational design to the decrees of Fate which govern Nature.

Pandulpho has realized the falseness of the stoic doctrine that man 'need only adhere to the dictates of right reason and he will be in harmony with a divinely and beneficently ordered scheme'.[2] It is

---

[1] Bertolt Brecht, *Gesammelte Werke*, 20 vols. (Frankfurt, 1967), 17, 947.

[2] G. D. Aggeler, 'Stoicism and Revenge in Marston', *English Studies*, 51 (1970), 511.

the absence of such a scheme which encourages relativism in morality:

> Most things that morally adhere to souls
> Wholly exist in drunk opinion,
> Whose reeling censure, if I value not,
> It values nought.
>
> (IV.i.31-4)

Suffering is not explained with reference to a wider moral order then, because none is available; man is 'confounded in a maze of mischief,/Stagger'd, stark fell'd with bruising stroke of chance' (IV.i.56-7).

There are, however, several references to heaven as a providential force. The first important example occurs in Antonio's description of the 'prodigies' he has seen. Viewing these, he says:

> I bow'd my naked knee and pierc'd the star
> With an outfacing eye, pronouncing thus:
> *Deus imperat astris.*
>
> (I.ii.121-3)

'God rules the stars': but does He? In the Christian tradition the stars were the instruments of Fortune while Fortune itself was under God's control. Antonio here reassures himself with an orthodoxy in which he later loses faith. Mellida similarly reassures herself of God's providential control:

> Heaven permits not taintless blood be spilt.
>
> (IV.i.151)

The death of the innocent Julio, already witnessed, gives the lie to this piety, and Mellida's own death is to follow. In fact, by the time she dies we are more inclined to see Fortune as a force independent of, not subordinate to, divine order. Everywhere Fortune is invoked to explain catastrophe and suffering; nowhere does anything occur that could be seen as the intervention of a beneficent deity. Moreover, both Piero and Strotzo exploit, for purposes of tyranny, the Christian idea of a deity administering retributive justice:

> *Strotzo*   Supreme Efficient,
> Why cleav'st thou not my breast with thunderbolts
> Of wing'd revenge?
>
> *Piero*   Why, art not great of thanks
> To gracious heaven for the just revenge
> Upon the author of thy obloquies?
>
> (IV.i.159–61; 214–16)

In the final sadistic revenge sequence, retributive providence and secular revenge are forcibly conjoined:

> *Andrugio*   Now down looks providence
> T'attend the last act of my son's revenge.
>
> (V.i.10–11)

This and other references like it (cf.v.ii.30; v.iii.67–8; v.iii.108–9) constitute perhaps the most problematic aspect of the play. Obviously there is no conceivable way that Christian theology could condone such revenge. It is true that Providence was thought to operate through evil agents, in effect, God using the sinful to destroy the sinful. This cannot be the case here, however, since Antonio and his accomplices not only survive, but are held in high esteem socially for what they have done.

We have to acknowledge that the fervid commitment to 'vengeance absolute' involves an ethic totally at odds with the religious absolute. Marston, fully aware that the one contravenes the other, forces them into an open disjunction in a deadly serious challenge to conventional providentialist dogma as it related to revenge. Providence has been discovered to be inoperative in a dislocated world where men destroy and alienate each other. Antonio and his accomplices overcome their alienation by associating as the bereaved and dispossessed and creating a sub-culture dedicated to violent revenge. As revengers, far from being the instrument of divine providence, they actually *take over* its retributive function, appropriating it with a gesture of defiance and deliberate sub-version:

Ghost of Andrugio I taste the joys of heaven,
Viewing my son triumph in his black blood.

Antonio Thus the hand of heaven chokes
The throat of murder. This for my father's blood.
He stabs Piero.

(v.iii.67–8; 108–9)

In thematic and theatrical terms the whole scene involves a process of ritual inversion: the marriage ceremony becomes a sadistic execution, the religious absolute is violated by 'vengeance abso-lute', the masque by the anti-masque, the decorum of the dance (*The Measure,* v.iii.49 S.D.) by the ritual torture of Piero (*They offer to run all at Piero, and on a sudden stop.* v.iii.105 S.D.)

The entire scene adds up to a subversion of providentialist orth-odoxy. As William R. Elton has demonstrated, the Elizabethan-Jacobean period witnessed 'the skeptical disintegration of provi-dential belief'.[1] This scene instances that disintegration, together with the dramatic structure appropriate for its expression. To understand that structure we need to see it in an historical context. The formal coherence of the morality play reflected the coherence of the metaphysical doctrine which was its principal subject. Dis-order and suffering are finally rendered meaningful through faith in, and experience of, a providential order. As *Everyman* puts it: God is a 'glorious fountaine, that all unclennes doth clarify'.[2] The best morality plays are anything but flatly didactic; they con-front, experientially, some of the deepest religious paradoxes. Nevertheless, they are paradoxes which are articulated through, and contained by, the same formal pattern: man exists in the shadow of original sin; he falls, suffers, and eventually repents; there is usually a relapse, incurring despair, before a secure recovery to redemption.

[1] William R. Elton, *King Lear and the Gods* (San Marino, California, 1966), 335.
[2] *Everyman,* in *Medieval Drama,* ed. David Bevington (Boston, 1975), 954, l. 545.

In Jacobean tragedy, the rejection of metaphysical harmony provokes the rejection of aesthetic harmony and the emergence of a new dialectic structure. Coherence now resides in the sharpness of definition given *to* metaphysical and social dislocation, not in an aesthetic, religious or didactic resolution *of* it.[1] Thus the alternative to such resolution is not necessarily 'irresolution' in the sense of intending, yet failing to dispose of contradictions. On the contrary, it may be that contradictory accounts of experience are forced into 'misalignment', the tension which this generates being a way of getting us to confront the problematic nature of reality itself.

So it is that in the final scene of *Antonio's Revenge* Marston subverts the dramatic conventions which embody a providentialist perspective. Through that subversion the perspective itself is 'deconstructed'.[2] In particular, the forced conjunction of the contradictory absolutes—secular and divine revenge—generates an internal strain which only stresses their actual disjunction.

The two themes which I have been exploring—the rejection of Christian-stoic accounts of identity and the subversion of providentialist orthodoxy—were closely linked in a period when both man and the world were undergoing radical re-definition. The sense that reality can no longer be adequately explained in terms of an in-forming absolute goes hand in hand with the realization that man cannot adequately define himself in terms of a fixed, unchanging essence. Thus, for Montaigne,

... *there is no constant existence, neither of our being, nor of the* *objects* [of experience]. And we, and our judgement, and all mortall things else do uncessantly rowle, turne and passe away.

[1] I discuss this more fully in 'Two Concepts of Mimesis: Renaissance Literary Theory and *The Revenger's Tragedy*', in *Themes in Drama*, ed. James Redmond (Cambridge, 1980), II, 25–47.

[2] I use the concept as in *OED*'s only citation of its use: 'A reform, the beginnings of which must be a work of deconstruction.' (McCarthy, 1882; *OED*, Compact Edition, p. 664.)

Moreover,

> We have no communication with being; for every humane
> nature is ever in the middle between being borne and dying;
> giving nothing of itselfe but an obscure apparence and shadow,
> and an uncertaine and weake opinion. And if perhaps you fix
> your thought to take its being; it would be even as if one should
> go about to grasp the water: for, how much the more he shal
> close and presse that, which by its owne nature is ever gliding,
> so much the more he shall loose what he would hold and fasten.
>
> (Montaigne, II, 323, my italics)

IV

Shakespeare, like Marston, explores the way in which the disintegrating effects of grief are resisted not through Christian or
stoic renunciation of society, but a commitment to revenge—a
vengeful re-engagement with the society and those responsible for
that grief. As in Marston it is a society which, like the wider
universe, has fallen into radical disharmony. In *Macbeth*, for
example, after Malcolm has told Macduff of the slaughter of his
wife and children, he adds,

> Be comforted,
> Let's make med'cines of our great revenge
> To cure this deadly grief.

> Let grief
> Convert to anger; blunt not the heart, enrage it.
> (IV.iii.213–15; 228–9)

Macduff's response to this invitation to 'cure' grief with brutal
revenge is revealing: he does indeed resort to revenge, but he
resists brutalization. Thus he insists that he will 'feel' as well as
'dispute' his grief (220–22), he refuses to kill Macbeth's mercen-
aries (v.vii.17–20) and he even offers Macbeth the opportunity of
being taken alive. He resists brutalization because his appalling
loss does not destroy, but rather confirms, his identity and purpose

as liberator of Scotland. And this is the role which sanctions, yet also moderates, his revenge. By contrast, Troilus, in *Troilus and Cressida*, turns to revenge to rescue himself from a collapse of identity and purpose; he, like Macduff, takes on the role of social revenger but, unlike Macduff, becomes brutalized in the process.

It is a difference accounted for in terms of the respective societies in which these individuals live. In each case it is society which confers on the individual his role of revenger, but they are societies with crucially different attitudes to violence: in *Macbeth* society approves the 'legalized' murder of the tyrant; in *Troilus* society approves senseless carnage—the 'Mad and fantastic execution' (v.v.38) in which Troilus submerges himself. To put it another way, in *Macbeth* war is seen generally as a social aberration; in *Troilus* it is the *raison d'être* of an 'heroic' society.

Once Troilus has witnessed what he sees as Cressida's betrayal he cannot again be the same person. Shattered idealism finds concentrated expression in that one disjunction: 'O beauty! Where is thy faith?' (v.ii.68).[1] Like Antonio he is brought to the edge of mental collapse (v.ii.137ff.) and, again like Antonio, he resists grief by taking on the role of revenger. Even his explanation for doing so resembles Antonio's: 'Hope of revenge shall hide our inward woe' (v.x.31). Troilus insists on going out to fight the final battle even though Hector tries to dissuade him. Hector thinks Troilus too young to die but Troilus scorns his concern:

> Let's leave the hermit pity with our mother;
> .... venomed vengeance ride upon our swords.
>
> (v.iii.45 and 47)

To which Hector replies: 'Fie, savage, fie!' Savage indeed, but that is exactly what Troilus has become.

The fate of Troilus is an ironic refutation of Agamemnon's account of 'grief' (i.iii.2) and its bracing effects on identity. He argues that the Greek's misfortunes have been

[1] *Troilus and Cressida*, New Cambridge Shakespeare, ed. Alice Walker (Cambridge, 1967).

> ... nought else
> But the protractive trials of great Jove
> To find persistive constancy in men ...
>
> (I.iii.19–21)

'Distinction', he adds,

> Puffing at all, winnows the light away,
> And what hath mass or matter, by itself
> Lies rich in virtue and unmingled.
>
> (I.iii.28–30)

To endure misfortune is to reveal one's true self—a pure essence of *virtù*—and, simultaneously, to discover that the universe is significantly ordered.

What happens to Troilus is the exact opposite: first, grief brings him to the very edge of mental collapse; second, he perceives the universe to be as devoid of order as his own life. Like Antonio he survives only by taking on the role of revenger and again the implication is clear: Troilus must depend for his identity and survival not on a stoical inner virtue but, quite simply, on his society; moreover, what his society is, he must ultimately become —that is, 'savage'. In a sense then, Troilus *has* become exactly what Agamemnon's true man, tempered by misfortune, should become: 'the thing of courage' which

> As roused with rage, with rage doth sympathize,
> And with an accent tuned in selfsame key
> Retorts to chiding fortune.
>
> (I.iii.52–4)

But this only intensifies the irony, especially if we recall that, at the very outset of the play, Troilus—anxious, immature but in love nevertheless—could dismiss the warmongers as 'Fools on both sides' (I.i.92). Now he is one of them, lover turned savage warrior, a thing of courage to whom mercy is 'a vice' (v.iii.37). Ulysses describes him in action:

> Troilus . . . hath done today
> Mad and fantastic execution,
> Engaging and redeeming of himself
> With such a careless force and forceless care . . .
>
> (v.v.37–40)

From the point of view of his society then, Troilus has become the heroic warrior. From another point of view he is only the thwarted lover rescuing himself from his own vulnerability by acting out a savage revenge.

In short, we see in both *Antonio's Revenge* and *Troilus and Cressida* the way that the sensitive individual brutalizes himself in order to survive in a brutal world. The irony or, as I prefer to think, the tragedy, lies in the fact that, in so doing, he earns the esteem of his society.

V

Troilus, in v.ii., is thrust into confrontation with a world which contradicts his, and others', idealization of it. His description of macrocosmic chaos is more than just a metaphorical declaration of his own disorientation. For Troilus to 'suffer into truth' is not to achieve tragic insight but rather to internalize the sense of contradiction which defines his world:

> Within my soul there doth conduce a fight
> Of this strange nature, that a thing inseparate
> Divides more wider than the sky and earth:
>
> The bonds of heaven are slipped, dissolved and loosed.
>
> (v.ii.145–7 and 154)

The scene is the climax of a play which, like *Antonio's Revenge*, not only disposes of the myth of a resilient human essence, but relentlessly undermines the related myth that the universe is providentially governed.

The setting of the play obviously precluded an explicitly

Christian form of providentialism. Instead Shakespeare uses natural law, the appropriate 'pagan' equivalent of Christian providentialism and, of course, one of its major sources. Briefly, natural law conceives of the universe as 'encoded' in creation with order, value and purpose. Man, in virtue of his rational capacity, synchronizes with this teleological design and discovers within it the main principles of his own moral law. Richard Hooker was the most celebrated Elizabethan exponent of such law; he constructed from it a version of Christian providentialism which was, arguably, the most persuasive ever.[1]

Troilus and Cressida has two prolonged philosophical debates, one in the Greek camp, primarily on order, the other in the Trojan camp, primarily on value. The main speech in each debate (by Ulysses and Hector respectively) embraces natural law and parallels quite closely passages from Hooker's *Laws*. Ulysses' famous 'degree' speech concentrates on hierarchical order in the universe and in human society: 'degree, priority and place ... in all line of order' (I.iii.86 and 88). It is 'neglection' of order 'That by a pace goes backward with a purpose/It hath to climb' (I.iii.128–9). Hector, in affirming the existence of 'moral laws/Of nature and of nations' (II.ii.184–5) captures the other essential tenet of natural law: human law derives from the pre-existent laws of nature; man discovers rather than makes social law. (The idea is fully elaborated in Hector's speech.)

Both of these appeals to natural law are contradicted elsewhere within the speeches in which they occur, and, moreover, by virtually all of the play's main themes. Thus Ulysses claims that order is encoded in nature yet simultaneously concedes that society is disordered and the universe in a state of incipient chaos. Additionally, there is a strong relativist tendency in Ulysses' speech[2] which runs exactly counter to the objectivism of natural law. Hector invokes in some detail the apparatus of natural law only to advocate action which flatly contradicts it (II.ii.189–93).

[1] Most notably, of course, in the first book of his *Of The Laws of Ecclesiastical Polity*.

[2] This is argued by William R. Elton in his article, 'Shakespeare's Ulysses and the Problem of Value', *Shakespeare Studies* II (1966), 95–111.

But this is only the beginning; thus, instead of hierarchical order there exists disintegration and chaos; instead of intrinsic purpose we find that

> Checks and disasters
> Grow in the veins of actions highest reared,
> As knots, by the conflux of meeting sap,
> Infects the sound pine and diverts his grain
> Tortive and errant from his course of growth.
>
> (I.iii.5–9)

The play is pervaded with imagery of this kind, again suggesting that in nature itself there is something which runs directly counter to the teleological harmony and integration of natural law.[1] Nature is presented as self-stultifying or paralysed by dislocated energies. The 'Tortive and errant ... growth' seems self-generated, and thwarted effort the consequence of effort itself:

> He that is proud eats up himself.
>
> (II.iii.153)

> O madness of discourse,
> That cause sets up with and against itself!
>
> (v.ii.142–3)

Disjunctions of this kind are central to the play's structure and, in this connection, Richard D. Fly has usefully analysed his sense of the play's 'imminent and radical chaos' in terms of its imitative form—that is, the 'disjunction in the plot, discontinuity in the scenario, inconsistency in characterization, dissonance, redundancy [and] lack of emphatic closure and resolution in Act V'.[2] Fly implies that chaos and 'universal cataclysm' (p. 291) is all that the play expresses. But there is much more happening. Characters repeatedly make positive or fatalistic appeals to an extra-human

---

[1] This repudiation of natural law is paralleled in *Antonio's Revenge*, especially in the speech of Pandulpho's (commented on above, p. 56), where he complains that 'all the strings of nature's symphony/Are crack'd and jar . . .'.

[2] Richard D. Fly, '"Suited in Like Conditions as our Argument": Imitative Form in Shakespeare's *Troilus and Cressida*', SEL 1500–1900, (1975), XV, 291.

reality or force: natural law, Jove, Chance, Time and so on. Philosophically all of these are very different from each other, but experientially they are almost interchangeable. The point is that they are all used to perpetuate a kind of false-consciousness which pervades the entire play. Thus, when Shakespeare undermines these appeals it is not from the impetus of nihilism alone; constantly he reveals both the false consciousness of his characters and the *social* reality for which they are constantly evading responsibility. One example must suffice.

It is customary to see the love of Troilus and Cressida as tragically destroyed by Time. To accept this view is to mystify the actual cause of separation: political exigency. Now, for Troilus, the cause is nothing less than divine interference:

> Cressid, I love thee in so strained a purity,
> That the blest gods, as angry with my fancy,
> More bright in zeal than the devotion which
> Cold lips blow to their deities, take thee from me.
>
> (IV.iv.24–7)

He goes on to blame 'Injurious Time' (42). The inconsistency only confirms that Troilus is not interested in exactly who or what is responsible, only in lifting responsibility from himself by displacing it into the realm of the beyond. It is a fatalism which effectively conceals, from himself as well as Cressida, his own passive complicity in the sacrifice of love to political expediency.

VI

It is widely accepted that in the Renaissance man rediscovered himself and the world. He shed the medieval insistence on human frailty and the world's corruption, affirming instead his vital and dynamic potential *in* the world. The Reformation ran counter to the Renaissance, yet shared with it this sense of man's centrality. And so, according to Raymond Williams, modern tragedy was born:

There is no important tragedy, within the Christian world, until there is also humanism and indeed individualism ... the release of personal energy, the emphasis of personal destiny which we can see, looking back, in the complex process of Renaissance and Reformation.[1]

The tragedy which Williams is describing involves a conflict between a surpassing individual and the forces which destroy him —'a tension between this thrust of the individual and an absolute resistance' (Williams, p. 87).

What emerges from this view of tragedy—I call it humanistic— is an obsessive concern with man's defeated potential, but it is the kind of defeat which only confirms the potential. Perhaps this is the significance of 'tragic waste': the forces destructive of life (fate, fortune, the gods or whatever) paradoxically pressure it into its finest expression in the events which lead to, and especially those which immediately precede, the protagonist's death. In one sense then we are talking about a potential which is, somehow, passively realized in its very defeat. We see, for example, men learning wisdom through suffering, men willing to know and endure their fate even as it destroys them. It may be that the individual, in virtue of his 'tragic flaw' is partly responsible for his suffering. Even so, the extent of his suffering is usually dispropor-tionate to his weakness (hubris, passion, ambition or whatever); to this extent he is more sinned against than sinning, and his potential is finally reaffirmed in his capacity to suffer with more than 'human' fortitude.

Alternatively, the protagonist's potential may be realized in a sacrificial sense, his death leading to the regeneration of his community—perhaps even of his universe.

Important and correct as this analysis may be for certain kinds of tragedy it seriously misrepresents plays like *Antonio's Revenge* and *Troilus and Cressida* and, I believe, many other major Jacobean tragedies. In those plays there is a powerful counter-tendency to the Renaissance-Reformation centralizing of man—a tendency, that is, to de-centre man, to push beyond the humanistic tragedy

[1] Raymond Williams, *Modern Tragedy*, revised edn. (London, 1979), 88.

of man's defeated potential to question the very existence of that potential. Antonio, Pandulpho and Troilus are 'heroes' who precisely lack that explicit or quasi-spiritual self-sufficiency (Christian or stoic) which is the source of the individual's tragic potential in humanistic tragedy as I have defined it. (The discrepancy between myth and actuality which identifies Hector, Ulysses and Achilles tells us that they too lack traditional heroic potential.)

There is something disturbingly honest in the fact that Antonio, Pandulpho and Troilus survive. The customary death of the tragic hero in humanistic tragedy seems, by contrast, to idealize or even mystify him. It is as if the greatness which was called into question is suddenly restored to him, abruptly put *beyond* question. Serious doubts of his potential as a surpassing individual are not confirmed by his death (revealing him as mere mortal) but are, rather, quietened by it, transformed into awe by its grandeur. Thus, somewhat paradoxically, tragic death may become a form of escapism, an evasion through mystifying closure of man's limitations.

In the two plays I have examined the protagonist survives suffering but at the cost of being brutalized by it and, moreover, defined by and dependent upon the social reality which has been responsible for it. Antonio, Pandulpho and Troilus internalize rather than transcend the violence of their society, being incapable of surviving its alienating effects except by re-engaging with it at all costs—the first two as kinds of terrorist-revengers, the third as a warrior-revenger.

Here then are the prototypes of the contradictory Jacobean anti-hero; he is malcontented—often because bereaved or dispossessed—satirical, and vengeful; he is at once agent and victim of social corruption, condemning yet simultaneously contaminated by it; he is made up of inconsistencies and contradictions which, because they cannot be understood in terms of individuality alone, pressure one's attention outwards to his society.

I have argued that this tendency in Jacobean drama to de-centre the individual is inseparable from its tendency to undermine Christian providentialism. Put the two things together and they comprise nothing less than a subversion of Christian humanism.

IV

Oxymoron and the Structure of Ford's 'The Broken Heart'

ANNE BARTON

AT the end of *The Broken Heart* (1627–31?) two unexpected deaths raise Nearchus, prince of Argos, to the throne of Sparta. The man who came to Sparta in Act III as a suitor for the hand of the Crown Princess Calantha remains there as Lacedaemonian king in his own right: chief mourner for a native, and now extinguished, royal house. Almost nothing that has happened in the last two acts was predictable. Nearchus admits as much in a concluding couplet:

> The counsels of the gods are never known
> Till men can call th'effects of them their own.[1]
>
> (v.iii.105–6)

Ford may well have been remembering Euripides. The Choruses of *Alcestis, Helen* and (with slight variations) *Medea, Andromache* and *Bacchae* all make the same statement at the end. Although human beings often pride themselves, mistakenly, on being able to anticipate their development, the plots devised by heaven are impenetrable until the final scene:

> Many are the forms of what is unknown.
> Much that the gods achieve is surprise.
> What we look for does not come to pass;
> God finds a way for what none forsaw.
> Such was the end of this story.[2]

[1] John Ford, *The Broken Heart*, ed. Donald K. Anderson Jr., Regents Renaissance Drama Series (London, 1968). All subsequent quotations from the play refer to this edition.

[2] Euripides, *Alcestis* and *Helen*, both trans. Richmond Lattimore, in *The Complete Greek Tragedies*, ed. David Grene and Richmond Lattimore (Chicago, 1955), ll. 1159–63, 1688–92.

In making this discovery, the Euripidean Chorus—like Nearchus later—speaks for the members of a disconcerted theatre audience.

The Broken Heart is the only one of Ford's plays set in a scrupulously maintained pagan world. The Sparta of Ithocles, Orgilus, Penthea and Calantha may exhibit a number of anachronistic Renaissance features: this icily passionate study in aristocratic stoicism (a tragedy without a villain, as it has been called)[1] rigorously excludes Christian reference. Its gods are frightening and opaque, speaking only in sinister riddles. Although the goodwill of Apollo and other deities is constantly being invoked, it rarely seems to manifest itself. Characters can be certain only of heaven's tireless surveillance and understanding of their most jealously guarded secrets. Armostes' melancholy realization that 'our eyes can never pierce into the thoughts,/For they are lodg'd too inward' (IV.i.17–18) is an experience common to all the men and women of the play. But heaven, as Euphranea says, 'does look into the secrets of all hearts' (I.i.113–14). Not even Tecnicus, the philosopher and servant of Apollo, can hope to rival the 'quick-piercing eyes' (I.iii.5) of these divine spies:

> Our mortal eyes
> Pierce not the secrets of your hearts; the gods
> Are only privy to them.
>
> (III.i.10–12)

In a society where virtually everyone but Bassanes conceals motivations and deep feelings fiercely and with great skill, such supernatural clairvoyance must be particularly disturbing. Remote and incomprehensible on their heights, the gods not only shape the action towards unforeseen conclusions, they see through the reticences, prevarications and disguised emotions of everyone else. It is precisely the position to which all the major characters of the tragedy aspire, and which not even Calantha can attain.

In another play, the omniscience of the gods might have been shared by the theatre audience. Ford, however, chose to turn the

---

[1] Roger T. Burbridge, 'The Moral Vision of Ford's *The Broken Heart*', *SEL* X (1970), 397.

very sophistication, the theatrical expertise of a group of habitual Caroline playgoers against them. To be well acquainted with Shakespeare, with the conventions of Elizabethan and Jacobean revenge tragedy, with standard character types and the normal configurations of plot within a five act structure is to be hindered, not helped, in understanding this play as it unfolds. Ford begins with a skilful recreation of the third scene of *Hamlet*. Here again is a young man embarking on a journey, taking leave of a testy and overly protective father while, at the same time, forbidding his sister to form an attachment of which he disapproves. But the parallel between Crotolon, Orgilus and Euphranea, and Polonius, Laertes and Ophelia is deliberately deceptive. Unlike Laertes, Orgilus has no intention of leaving home. He surprises the audience two scenes later by turning up, disguised, in the palace gardens. There, he puts on something remarkably like Hamlet's antic disposition, and is employed by the unsuspecting Prophilus, Euphranea's lover, to carry letters between the two, in secret, 'at nine i' th' morning and at four at night' (I.iii.155). Any audience watching Prophilus and Euphranea fall into this trap, and hearing the ominous soliloquy with which Orgilus concludes the scene, might be forgiven for feeling confident about the direction that the action is going to take:

> Put out thy torches, Hymen, or their light
> Shall meet a darkness of eternal night.
> Inspire me, Mercury, with swift deceits;
> Ingenious fate has leapt into my arms,
> Beyond the compass of my brain.
>
> (I.iii.175–9)

It comes as a shock to discover, not only that no love-letters ever materialize upon which Orgilus can exercise his 'swift deceits', but that two acts later he will freely bestow his sister upon Prophilus, his enemy's best friend, and wish the bridal pair nothing more sinister than 'comforts lasting, loves increasing' (III.iv.70).

Kenneth Muir has recently complained about two 'structural faults' in *The Broken Heart*: first, the 'clumsy' way in which

Penthea is left in the palace garden to await her brother but, when Ithocles is suddenly taken ill, finds herself confronting Orgilus, her former affianced lover, instead; and, secondly, the abrupt shift of focus on to Calantha at the end.[1] But, arguably, such *non sequiturs* are deliberate, the dramatic principle upon which the entire tragedy is based. Ford is calculatedly evasive as to just where, among Penthea, Calantha, Orgilus, Ithocles, Amyclas, Nearchus and even Bassanes, his tragic centre lies. Interest is diffused among the different members of a society: an aristocratic social order whose well-being is ultimately more important than that of any of its components. This kind of structure possesses obvious affinities with that of comedy. And indeed, despite the brooding presence of Orgilus, it is by no means clear at first that the material of *The Broken Heart* must necessarily be tragic.

If the opening scene summons up memories of *Hamlet*, its successor immediately subverts the prognostication by suggesting the jubilant early stages of *Much Ado About Nothing*. A war has been triumphantly concluded, and its returning heroes are clearly ripe for falling in love and re-populating the world they have just diminished. The old king of Sparta feels himself transformed and 'ent'ring/Into his youth again' (I.ii.4–5). Lord Ithocles, described in the first scene as 'insulting' (50), a man 'proud of youth,/And prouder in his power' (39–40), turns out to be a victorious general of great modesty and tact. Groneas and Hemophil, the two courtiers-turned-soldier, initiate a subsidiary comic intrigue when they resolve to ignore Christalla and Philema in future, instead of pursuing them, and hope that then 'they'll follow us' (147). Even Bassanes, the jealous monster introduced at the beginning of Act II, arouses comic expectations through his unabashed derivation from Jonson's Kitely and Corvino, and (to a lesser extent) Shakespeare's Ford.

All of these comedy expectations prove false. Despite Amyclas' own confidence that his life is renewing itself—'It will, it must' (I.ii.10)—and in the midst of rumours that the rejuvenated king has grown a new beard of 'a pure carnation colour' (II.i.47), the

---

[1] Kenneth Muir, 'The Case of John Ford', in *The Sewanee Review* LXXXIV (1976), 623–4.

old man suddenly sickens and dies. Ithocles, although not to be contained within the hostile and simplistic description offered by Orgilus in the opening scene, still has more than a trick of the old self-centred arrogance about him. When he displays it in Act IV, the consequences are fatal. The putative intrigue involving Groneas, Hemophil and Calantha's two maids of honour breaks off, perplexingly, in scene two, exactly where it began. It is never heard of again. In her final testament, Calantha arbitrarily disposes of Christalla as wife to Nearchus' friend Amelus, and sends Philema into perpetual seclusion as a vestal virgin. Considering that their names, as Ford points out in the list of *dramatis personae*, mean 'Crystal' and 'A Kiss' respectively, one might think that these destinies ought more appropriately to have been reversed. Calantha, however, appears to be a dramatist as perverse as Ford himself. As for Bassanes, he contradicts his apparent comic type by becoming, first, a genuinely tragic figure as he contemplates the wreck of Penthea's sanity, and then ending the play as the newly created Marshal of Sparta, an infinitely sadder but also transformed man at whom nobody is any longer tempted to laugh.

Five deaths dispersed through Acts IV and V make the final movement of *The Broken Heart* unequivocally tragic. The pattern, however, is one that both summons up and obstinately refuses to conform to the requirements and expectations of the traditional revenge play. Even as the paradigm of *Romeo and Juliet* lurks behind *'Tis Pity She's A Whore*, making the star-crossed love of Giovanni and Annabella something that it is impossible either to endorse or condemn, so *The Broken Heart* uses *The Spanish Tragedy, Hamlet*, and their Jacobean successors to deceive the theatre audience about Orgilus and his function in the action. Misleading clues and cunningly laid false trails gesture towards a kind of shadow revenge tragedy always promising to emerge through the fabric of the unconventional one Ford actually wrote. In this ghost play Orgilus, disguised as the poor scholar Aplotes, not only uses his role as go-between to trouble the love of Prophilus and Euphranea, he inflames Nearchus' jealousy of Ithocles until the prince takes steps to ensure that 'low mushrooms never rival cedars' (IV.i.98). Penthea's self-control does not survive her

encounter with Orgilus in the garden. The woman who can so
fervently invoke 'wild fires' (III.ii.47) to scorch, before they finally
consume, her brother's heart, in retribution for what he has made
of her life, is surely not going to plead his love-suit to Calantha.

Most striking of all, perhaps, is the indication that Orgilus, like
so many Elizabethan and Jacobean revengers, will bring his
purposes to fruition in a deceiving show:

> If these gallants
> Will please to grace a poor invention
> By joining with me in some slight device,
> I'll venture on a strain my younger days
> Have studied for delight.
>
> (III.iv.84–8)

It might be Kyd's Hieronymo assembling his unsuspecting actors
for the slaughter. When Groneas, Hemophil and Ithocles all
volunteer to take part in Orgilus' device to honour the nuptials of
Prophilus and Euphranea, the knowledgeable theatre audience
primes itself for the holocaust. The 'Soliman and Perseda' play at
the end of *The Spanish Tragedy*, the fencing match in *Hamlet*, and
the barriers at court in *The White Devil*, the murderous masques
of *The Revenger's Tragedy*, Middleton's *Women Beware Women*,
and Marston's *Antonio's Revenge* (not to mention Hippolyta's
lethal contribution to the wedding feast in Ford's own '*Tis Pity*)
all lend their weight to the supposition that, as so often in the past,
the 'entertainment' will explode into violence. Alert members of
the audience, remembering Prophilus' early claim that Ithocles
was a friend 'in whom the period of my fate consists' (I.ii.42)
might even expect the bridegroom to join Ithocles and the other
amateur actors in the list of victims.

Every one of these clues is false. The course of Prophilus' and
Euphranea's love runs smoothly to its happy conclusion. Nearchus,
once he is convinced that Calantha returns Ithocles' passion,
magnanimously withdraws his own suit:

> ... affections injur'd
> By tyranny or rigor of compulsion,

Like tempest-threaten'd trees unfirmly rooted,
Ne'er spring to timely growth.

(IV.ii.205–8)

He will only pretend to be jealous 'of what privately I'll further'
(IV.ii.211). Penthea, forgetting her own wrongs, bravely speaks
for her brother to Calantha, and earns a royal rebuke. Orgilus
presents no show at his sister's wedding. Before the revels begin,
he has caught Ithocles in the imprisoning chair and killed him. It
is a 'device' of a kind, but scarcely to be identified with the 'strain
my younger days have studied' which Orgilus offered back in
Act III, and it has no audience apart from the dead Penthea. The
'shows' of Act V turn out to be the formal court dance which
Calantha refuses to interrupt for tidings of calamity, Orgilus'
ritual suicide—described by Bassanes as though it were halfway to
being a work of art (V.ii.131–4)—and its complement and correct-
ive: the supreme effort of will through which Calantha transforms
her coronation into a wedding which is also a funeral.

In the epilogue to *The Broken Heart*, Ford briefly borrowed the
voice of Ben Jonson:

> Where noble judgments and clear eyes are fix'd
> To grace endeavor, there sits truth not mix'd
> With ignorance. Those censures may command
> Belief which talk not till they understand.

(1–4)

Ford's insistence that his aim was 'well to deserve of *all*, but please
the *best*' (12), like his plea that no one should presume to criticize
before they 'understand', recalls the arrogant Jonson of *Cynthia's
Revels, Poetaster*, and the two addresses to the reader prefixed to
Catiline. On the other hand, his prediction of a contradictory and
confused response to *The Broken Heart* reflects the problems posed
specifically by his own play. This tragedy, Ford seems to be
saying, will not be easy to decode. Indeed, different members of
the audience may well end up by criticizing it for what seem to be
mutually exclusive faults:

Let some say, 'This was flat'; some, 'Here the scene
Fell from its height'; another, that the mean
Was 'ill observ'd' in such a growing passion
As it transcended either state or fashion.

(5–8)

Apparently, *The Broken Heart* is vulnerable to the charges of being
flat and dull, but also sensational, feverish, and over-wrought.

Ford was shrewd. The warring responses which he anticipated
in his epilogue have been perpetuated in the critical history of this
play. *The Broken Heart* has regularly been accused of flatness, what
Robert Ornstein once described as 'pallor' and other critics have
seen as a puzzling monotony of plot and character.[1] Conversely,
it has been felt to be exaggerated and shrill: a decadent study in
extreme and implausible emotional states, which employs excessive and elliptical forms of speech. The possibility that both reactions might point towards intrinsic qualities of the play, antinom-
ies explored and ultimately reconciled within it, has proved more
difficult to entertain. Yet this is surely the solution to the riddle
posed by Ford's epilogue: the 'strain' which those who 'understand' are asked to countenance and allow, so that 'the *Broken
Heart* may be piec'd up again' (14). The tragedy is like that poem
which Yeats hoped one day to offer his Connemara fisherman:
'cold and passionate as the dawn'.[2]

The rhetorical term *oxymoron*, although not noted by the OED
before 1640, was probably known in England before that date. It
occurs in fourth-century Latin commentaries on Virgil, in its
present sense: a figure by which 'contradictory terms are conjoined so as to give point to the statement or expression' (OED).
Although rhetoricians also employed *conciliatio* in a similar fashion, the latter term tended to be reserved for verbal structures
larger than a mere noun and its modifier. *Oxymoron* is an interesting word because it enacts its own meaning. Two antithetical

---

[1] Robert Ornstein, *The Moral Vision of Jacobean Tragedy* (Madison, Wiscon-
sin), 213.
[2] Charles O. McDonald has used this line from Yeats's poem 'The Fisherman,
to describe *The Broken Heart*, in 'The Design of John Ford's *The Broken Heart*',
SP LIX (1962), 157.

words, ὀξός (*sharp*) and μωρός (*dull*) are rammed together in a way that forces reappraisal of each. It is tempting to speculate that Ford may have had the term *oxymoron* specifically in mind when he prophesied disagreement among his audience, in the epilogue, as to whether *The Broken Heart* ought to be castigated for being too high-pitched, or for being dull. Certainly the play makes repeated and striking use of the figure. Most of these oxymorons are generated by the predicament of Penthea, the irresolvable dilemma at the heart of the tragedy, and by the consequent behaviour of Orgilus. But the figure is central to *The Broken Heart* as a whole: the most intense and undiluted way of expressing the contradictoriness of life in this society, and something of its sense of claustrophobia and impasse.

The Broken Heart is the only one of Ford's plays which does not relax into a single line of prose. Even Phulas and Grausis, Bassanes' retainers and the only non-aristocratic characters in the tragedy, speak verse. In general, the language of the play gravitates towards paradox. Ithocles is 'a friend/Firm and unalterable. But a brother/More cruel than the grave' (I.iii.62-3). Penthea, 'old in griefs' and yet 'in years . . . a child' (III.v.50-51), is one 'buried in a bridebed' (II.ii.38). Her husband Bassanes, whose uxorious passion is 'nurse unto a fear so strong and servile' (I.i.62), discovers by possessing Penthea that 'the way to poverty is to be rich' (II.i.70). Orgilus defines himself as 'no brave yet no unworthy enemy' (V.ii.139), and the newly created Marshal of Sparta, contemplating Calantha at the end, finds that he 'must weep to see/ Her smile in death' (V.iii.97-8). That Apollo's oracle at Delphi should speak in riddles—'The lifeless trunk shall wed the broken heart', and 'Revenge proves its own executioner' (IV.i.134-139)— is only to be expected; less predictable is the compulsion felt by virtually all the characters towards verbal compression, towards the unmediated and painful confrontation of warring terms.

Compound and hyphenated words are a feature of *The Broken Heart*. The 'lover-bless'd heart' (III.ii.45) of 'life-spent Penthea' has been ground into dust by 'death-braving Ithocles' (I.ii.11). The 'monster-love' of Bassanes leads him to accuse his wife of living in 'swine-security of bestial incest' (III.ii.150) with her own brother.

Ithocles dies into a 'long-look'd-for peace' (IV.iv.70). It may be that the unusual frequency of such compounds in this play is another indication of Ford's scrupulosity about his Spartan setting: he must have known that the tendency 'to peece many words together to make of them one entire, much more significative than the single word', had been stressed by Puttenham and other rhetoricians of the period as characteristic of the ancient Greeks.[1] A few of the compound words in *The Broken Heart* (e.g. 'monster-love') gesture towards the condition of oxymoron. Essentially, however, they imply unity and equivalence, of a perilous and uneasy kind. In this sense they are unlike those stifling noun/adjective relationships through which the genuine incompatibilities of the play are expressed: 'noble shame' (IV.ii.150), 'excellent misery' v.ii.66), 'dreadful safety' (v.ii.117), 'married bachelors' (v.ii.131), 'honourable infamy' (v.ii.123), or Penthea's own description of herself as 'a ravish'd wife/Widow'd by lawless marriage' (IV.ii.146–7).

The work of Glenn Blayney and Peter Ure on the status of formal betrothals in the sixteenth and seventeenth centuries has at least rescued Penthea from the old critical charge of being some kind of hysterical Platonic: a girl who conceals her fundamental abhorrence of sex behind an exaggerated notion of the importance of her previous contract with Orgilus.[2] In fact, her position resembles that of Clare in Wilkins's *Miseries of Enforced Marriage* (1606), after her affianced lover has yielded to family pressure and married someone else:

> A wretched maid, not fit for any man,
> For being united his with plighted faiths,
> Whoever sues to me commits a sinne,
> Besiedgeth me, and who shal marry me:
> Is like my selfe, lives in Adultery, (O God)
> That such hard Fortune, should betide my youth.

[1] George Puttenham, *The Arte of English Poesie*, ed. G. D. Willcock and A. Walker (Cambridge, 1936), 156–7.
[2] Glenn Blayney, 'Enforcement of Marriage in English Drama 1600–1650, in' *PQ* XXXVIII (1959), 459–72. Peter Ure, 'Marriage and the Domestic Drama in Heywood and Ford', *ES* XXXII (1951), 200–16.

> I am Young, Fayre, Rich, Honest, Virtuous,
> Yet for all this, who ere shall marry mee
> I am but his whore, live in Adultery ...
> I must be made a strumpet gainst my will.[1]

Wilkins's heroine finally stabs herself to avoid such a fate; Penthea, in *The Broken Heart*, actually experiences it. Both of her contracts, the one with Orgilus solemnized in the presence of her father, and the 'noble shame' of her enforced marriage to the wealthy Lord Bassanes, are legally and emotionally binding. Each one contaminates and nullifies the other. She behaves to both men with extraordinary probity and restraint, but the situation itself is intolerable, and would be so even if Bassanes were not a jealous lunatic. The cruelty of Ithocles has created a 'divorce betwixt my body and my heart' (II.iii.57), condemning Penthea to live out a kind of perpetual and agonizing Marvellian 'Dialogue Between the Soul and Body', in which the two partners perpetually accuse and torment one another.

When a penitent Ithocles foresees that his sister will become a martyr to whom 'married wives' (III.ii.85) direct their orisons, the apparent redundancy of his formulation is purposeful and telling. It reflects his belated awareness that, thanks to him, this is not in fact Penthea's condition. Addressing Calantha later, Penthea plays pathetically with the epithets 'virgin wives' and 'married maids' (III.v.52, 56), beneficent oxymorons which express a Spenserian ideal of purity and chastity within the married state. Her own position, as she knows, is that of chaste whore and 'ravish'd wife'. It cannot be maintained. Calantha's disingenuous, if understandable, snub when Penthea tries to win her for Ithocles snaps a sanity and will already stretched to breaking point. Penthea gives way to the anorexic's 'terrified passion for purity', to that 'dilemma of the self whose boundaries feel infinitely vulnerable to invasion from surrounding territory, either because of some constitutional fragility, or insensitive impingement from

---

[1] George Wilkins, *The Miseries of Enforced Marriage*, Tudor Facsimile Texts, ed. John S. Farmer (London, 1913) C4V.

the environment, or both'.[1] She puts an end to the warfare between body and heart by choosing to punish the former for its
involuntary corruption:

> Penthea's, poor Penthea's name is strumpeted.
> But since her blood was season'd by the forfeit
> Of noble shame with mixtures of pollution,
> Her blood ('tis just) be henceforth never heighten'd
> With taste of sustenance. Starve; let that fullness
> Whose pleurisy hath fever'd faith and modesty—
> Forgive me. O, I faint!
>
> (IV.ii.148–54)

Psychologically, the reaction is entirely comprehensible. Its consequences, however, are tragic in a way Penthea herself did not
foresee.

When Orgilus tells Bassanes, in Act IV, that Penthea 'is left a
prey to words' (IV.ii.44), he surely does not mean (as one of the
play's recent editors would have it) that the insanity which afflicts
her in her last hours exposes her to 'scandal'.[2] The line is both more
literal and more far-reaching. Once 'the empress of her soul, her
reason' (IV.ii.48) has been deposed, Penthea becomes the victim of
all those turbulent feelings of love and hate, of that desire for
vengeance, which she has suppressed so gallantly up to this point.
The woman whose conscious will forbade her to repay the
insufferable Bassanes in kind, to encourage Orgilus' passion in the
garden, or to revenge herself on her brother when the opportunity
offered itself, is now left 'a prey to words' which her rational and
waking mind would never have permitted her to utter.

Once again, and at a crucial moment in the play, Ford was
remembering *Hamlet*. Ophelia too not only exposed a carefully
concealed private self in her madness ('To-morrow is Saint
Valentine's day'), she whetted Laertes's desire to be revenged on
Prince Hamlet—something from which her conscious mind would
have recoiled. Ophelia directs no blame towards the man she

---

[1] Rosemary Dinnage, reviewing three clinical books on anorexia in *The New
York Review of Books*, 22 February 1979, 8.
[2] D. K. Anderson, *op. cit.*, 75.

loves. But Laertes, as he watches her distribute her pathetic flowers, puts words into her mouth: 'Hadst thou thy wits and didst persuade revenge,/It could not move thus'.[1] Penthea, whose roses were all gathered in Act II, does make an accusation. Pointing to her brother Ithocles, she summons up the ghost of her ruined happiness and reminds Orgilus of who destroyed it: 'that is he . . . that's he, and still 'tis he' (IV.ii.115, 122). And Orgilus, a potential revenger who has recently seemed to waver in his purpose, finds that

> She has tutor'd me;
> Some powerful inspiration checks my laziness . . .
> If this be madness, madness is an oracle.
>
> (IV.ii.124–5, 133)

From this moment on, the tragedy is inevitable in human as well as divine terms. It is a tragedy made more poignant because the magnanimous and loving Penthea, when sane, would have done anything to prevent it. Her madness has produced a different kind of divorce between body and heart, unleashing all the weaknesses and passionate, vindictive impulses which her conscious emotional self had overcome at such crippling cost.

For Orgilus too, Ithocles' arrogant violation of the pre-contract has resulted in a divorce between body and heart:

> All pleasures are but mere imagination,
> Feeding the hungry appetite with steam
> And sight of banquet, whilst the body pines,
> Not relishing the real taste of food.
> Such is the leanness of a heart divided
> From intercourse of troth-contracted loves.
>
> (II.iii.34–9)

Like Penthea, Orgilus can find no way out of the impasse, except through the creation of a body/heart division of another kind. When Orgilus betrays Ithocles at last, kills him, and so avenges

[1] William Shakespeare, *Hamlet*, in The Riverside Shakespeare, ed. G. Blakemore Evans *et. al.* (Boston, 1974), IV.v. 169–70.

his own and Penthea's wrongs, he is a man divided in his feelings about the act as no previous revenger had been in sixteenth-and seventeenth-century drama. His hesitations are not Hamlet's, nor are they the compunctions of the hero in Marston's *Antonio's Revenge*, before he murders the inoffensive little son of his enemy Piero. Tecnicus' rejection of the revenge code as an example of false honour has touched his pupil not at all. Orgilus not only nurses an acute sense of personal injury, he believes that the martyred Penthea has given him a mandate to kill. Unfortunately, he also finds when the moment of decision comes that he admires and respects his victim.

It is true that the selfishness of Ithocles, after Calantha has accepted him as her husband on a pre-contract, makes it easier for Orgilus to proceed:

> *Orgilus*   I was myself a piece of suitor once,
>   And forward in preferment too; so forward
>   That, speaking truth, I may without offence, sir,
>   Presume to whisper that my hopes and, hark'ee,
>   My certainty of marriage stood assured
>   With as firm footing, by your leave, as any's
>   Now at this very instant—but—
> *Ithocles*   'Tis granted.
>   And for a league of privacy between us,
>   Read o'er my bosom and partake a secret:
>   The princess is contracted mine.
>
> (IV.iii.113–22)

Ithocles' interruption is grossly insensitive in itself. Even worse is the way he brushes aside the parallel between Orgilus' blighted expectation of happiness and his own, present anticipation of joy. Orgilus will remind Ithocles later of this lapse, of how his rapture at the prospect of enjoying Calantha and a crown not only made him neglect Penthea's sufferings, but rendered 'my injuries . . . beneath your royal pity' (IV.iv.36–7). Even before he stabs Ithocles, however, Orgilus has begun to prove the truth of his prisoner's cool injunction: 'On to the execution, and inherit/A conflict with thy horrors' (IV.iv.50–51).

Revengers in seventeenth-century drama do not usually take their victims' hands in token of heart-felt regard before delivering the fatal blow, encourage them during their death-throes, and praise them dead. Orgilus bids Ithocles farewell as 'fair spring of manhood' (IV.iv.71), and couples him with Penthea: 'Sweet twins, shine stars forever' (IV.iv.74). He is a revenger emptied of rancour, his action almost as mechanical as the chair he uses to guarantee success, and he is quietly resolved on his own death. Not for an instant does he consider the 'dreadful safety' of flight, so magnanimously recommended by his dying enemy. Instead, he seeks out Calantha at once and confesses that 'brave Ithocles is murder'd, murder'd cruelly' (v.ii.16). Orgilus never admits that his reasons for killing Ithocles were anything but 'just and known' (v.ii.46). He does not regret what he has done. He simply divorces the almost impersonal necessity for the action, as he sees it, from what he acknowledges to be the butchery (v.ii.41) of its accomplishment, and the worth of his victim: 'Never liv'd gentleman of greater merit,/Hope, or abiliment to steer a kingdom' (v.ii.47–8). Once again, the only resolution of this conflict, of the 'honorable infamy' (v.ii.123) of Orgilus' condition, lies in death.

In an essay called 'The Task of Cultural History', Johan Huizinga once tried to distinguish between what he called aristocratic and popular cultures:

An aristocratic culture does not advertise its emotions. In its forms of expression it is sober and reserved. Its general attitude is stoic. In order to be strong it wants to be and needs to be hard and unemotional, or at any rate to allow the expression of feelings and emotions only in elegant forms ... The populace is always anti-stoic. Great waves of emotion, floods of tears, and excesses of feeling have always been breaks in the dikes of the popular soul, which then usually swept away the spirit of the upper classes.[1]

[1] Johan Huizinga, *Men and Ideas: Essays on History, the Middle Ages, the Renaissance*, trans. James S. Holmes and Hans van Marle, (New York, 1970), 48–9.

Racine comes most immediately to mind as the dramatist of a tragic aristocracy struggling against overwhelming odds to subdue or at least shape its passionate emotions. But he was anticipated by Ford in *The Broken Heart*. The play has in common with *Phèdre* or *Bérénice* a sense of almost unendurable repression, of torrents of feeling made to flow in channels too narrow and constricted to contain them. Explosion is always imminent, a violation of decorum which will shake this world apart. The code which governs Spartan society demands that people should maintain a rigid self-control. Because these characters are all passionate by nature, and because their situations either are or become extreme, such control is possible only through various forms of self-imposed psychological violence. The outward stillness towards which everyone but Bassanes strives is excruciatingly difficult to maintain. The lava crust is thin on the top of the volcano and, when the explosion comes, it tends to be all the more devastating because it has for so long been held artificially in check.

Book in hand, the conscious replica of Hamlet mad in craft, Orgilus disguised as the scholar Aplotes had bestowed upon his sister and Prophilus in Act I a 'distracted' meditation with method in it:

> Say it: is it possible
> With a smooth tongue, a leering countenance,
> Flattery, or force of reason—I come t'ee, sir—
> To turn or to appease the raging sea?
> Answer to that. Your art? What art to catch
> And hold fast in a net the sun's small atoms?
> No, no; they'll out; ye may as easily
> Outrun a cloud driven by a northern blast
> As fiddle-faddle so. Peace, or speak sense.
>
> (I.iii.102–10)

The speech recognizes the potency of powerful, uncivilized forces. Like the sun, the sea and the wind, human emotions naturally evade regulation and capture—whether in the form of Tecnicus' rational counsels, or (more painfully) the attempts of individuals to conform to a demanding aristocratic code. In itself, this code is neither arid nor ridiculous. It governs Tecnicus' rigorous but compassionate surveillance of them all, and his rejection of revenge as untidy and irrational, the dignity with which King Amyclas accepts the fact that he is not about to regain his youth after all, but to die, Nearchus' generous renunciation of Calantha, and the 'undaunted spirit' (v.ii.42) of Ithocles when facing the death of a trapped animal. It also dictates Penthea's irreproachable behaviour to Orgilus, to her brother Ithocles, and to the husband who makes her life a hell. At the end of the play, Calantha will bring it to the point of apotheosis: a vindication made even more impressive because she alone forges a wholeness and rapport between Sparta's social ideal and the heart's truth. That is why she, and not Penthea, is ultimately the heroine of *The Broken Heart*.

Although Orgilus has threatened from the beginning to tear through and destroy the ideals of his class, it is the nobleman Bassanes who provides the fullest and most depressing exposition of what Ford sees in this play as the alternative. When he appears for the first time in Act II, talking of ear-wigs, warts, pimples, city housewives, hounds' heads, wag-tails and jays, bitch-foxes, bedposts and collops, he introduces a language alien to that spoken by anyone else in the play. This is partly because of its unremitting lowness and physicality, partly because of a specificity which throws into relief the other characters' predilection for the abstract. Bassanes' speech, like his imagination, is populated with monsters of his own invention: horned beasts, nightmares, rotten maggots, human beings with the features of dogs, cats, foxes and swine, and 'the deformed bear-whelp/Adultery' (ii.i.5–6). For those around him, he is himself a freak of nature. Orgilus, attempting to describe Bassanes' schizoid attitude towards his wife, calls it 'monster-love' (i.i.61). Ithocles, when accused of incest with Penthea, flings the epithet 'monster' at Bassanes (iii.ii.154) and, even for his servant Grausis, he is an 'animal' (iii.ii.178).

Not until he has been forcibly separated from the wife he both adores and reviles can Bassanes see that he is himself a beast more hideous than anything his diseased mind has been able to conjure up: 'of those beasts/The worst am I' (iv.ii.28–9). Purified by this recognition, his language now takes on an abstract quality and dignity like that of the other characters. From being the one inhabitant of the court wholly incapable of controlling his passions, a man accustomed to vent all his private emotions and fears, he moves to an extreme of stoicism in the face of disaster:

> Make me the pattern of digesting evils,
> Who can outlive my mighty ones, not shrinking
> At such a pressure as would sink a soul
> Into what's most of death, the worst of horrors.
> But I have seal'd a covenant with sadness,
> And enter'd into bonds without condition,
> To stand these tempests calmly.—Mark me, nobles,
> I do not shed a tear, not for Penthea.
> Excellent misery!
>
> (v.ii.58–69)

The culminating oxymoron makes it plain that Bassanes' new attitude is agonizing and, in a sense, unnatural. But this excruciating self-restraint, a forcible subordination of passion to the dictates of reason and the will, is preferable to the hysteria and self-indulgence of his earlier self. Restored to his rightful place in Sparta's aristocratic society, Bassanes ceases to be an aberrant, comic character.

Amid the pure, consciously restricted diction of *The Broken Heart*, 'monsters' acquire something of the prominence and special significance that the word *monstre* possesses in *Phèdre*. Ithocles humbly admits to the sister he has wronged that 'ingratitude of nature/Hath made my actions monstrous' (III.ii.81–2). Armostes fears that his nephew's ambition for Calantha's hand will result in some prodigious birth, like the centaur Ixion fathered on a cloud (IV.i.69–73). The mad Penthea's imagination runs on sirens, half woman, half bird. Her desperate resolution to starve herself will tempt Nature to 'call her daughter monster' (IV.ii.156). Orgilus is rumoured to have fled to Athens on a fiery dragon (II.i.54), and to have returned to Sparta through the agency of hobgoblins (III.iv.36). Meeting him after the secret murder of Ithocles, Bassanes is uniquely and tellingly impelled to revert to the disordered language he employed before his reformation:

I will not aught to do with thee of all men.
The doublers of a hare; or, in a morning,
Salutes from a splay-footed witch . . .
Are not so boding mischief as thy crossing
My private meditations. Shun me, prithee.

(v.i.11–13, 16–17)

Here, for once, the monstrosity Bassanes senses is actual, and not merely a product of his own diseased imagination.

However it manifests itself, the monstrous is at odds with Sparta's rational, demanding aristocratic ideal. Revenge, whether it takes the form of Orgilus' futile murder, or Ithocles' earlier revival of an obsolete family feud, is monstrous: a false honour, 'proceeding from the vices of our passion,/Which makes our reason drunk' (iii.i.36–7). Penthea's collapse into inanition and lunacy, however pathetic and understandable under the circumstances, is nonetheless grotesque, a surrender to the irrational which proves horribly destructive to the people she most loves. As *The Broken Heart* nears its ending, Ford poises against these failures a number of triumphs: the self-control of Nearchus, the way Ithocles and Amyclas face death, the redemption of Bassanes and, most memorable of all, Calantha's demonstration of the fundamental strength and cohesion of this social order, when she refuses to shatter the formal patterns of the courtly dance for the individual deaths of her father, her friend Penthea, and her affianced lord.

Like *Antony and Cleopatra* and *The Duchess of Malfi*, *The Broken Heart* possesses a divided catastrophe.[1] Where Shakespeare and Webster had drawn the line of demarcation between Acts IV and V, Ford chose to contain it within Act V. The effect, however, is the same. An apparent climax, an expected ending, is set up and then denied. The tragedy surprises its audience by continuing, and by doing so in a way that forces a radical re-adjustment of attitudes, and a perspective on the action, that had seemed settled. Calantha has consistently been the most opaque and unknowable

[1] See the present writer's discussion of the divided catastrophe as a dramatic device in 'Nature's Piece 'gainst Fancy': The Divided Catastrophe in 'Antony and Cleopatra', Bedford College Inaugural Lecture (London, 1972).

of the major characters in the play. Only two small hints—her choice of Ithocles rather than Nearchus to lead her off-stage at III.iv.75–6, and the ambiguous business with the ring at IV.i.25–34 —have betrayed the inner workings of her heart. Penthea goes to her death believing that her love embassy has failed. When, in Act IV, Calantha ceremoniously asks her father to give her Ithocles for her own, the old king obviously believes that she is assuring him of favour in what will shortly be the new reign. He does not realize that he has just given parental sanction to a pre-contract which cuts out the Prince of Argos. For the theatre audience, however, which overhears Calantha's aside to Ithocles, 'Th'art mine.—Have I now kept my word?' (IV.iii.87), the shock is considerable. It becomes plain that in a scene Ford has high-handedly refused to show us, these two have made a mutual declaration of love. They stand before us as a betrothed couple, although just how they have arrived at this understanding remains unclear. Ithocles' passion for Calantha, strong enough to make him sicken physically, as well as possessing his mind, has been amply displayed. The nature and depth of her feelings for him are altogether less certain. In the absence of the betrothal scene itself, the answer seems to be provided by her behaviour in the dance.

Meditating on ambition in the specific context of what then seemed to be his hopeless passion for Calantha, Ithocles in Act II had reflected that

> Morality applied
> To timely practice keeps the soul in tune,
> At whose sweet music all our actions dance.
> But this is form of books and school tradition;
> It physics not the sickness of a mind
> Broken with griefs.
>
> (II.ii.8–13)

Like Orgilus in the habit of Aplotes, Ithocles impatiently rejects the rational ideal honoured in Sparta as something inadequate in practice, however persuasive in the abstract. Calantha, by contrast, turns the abstraction of Ithocles' fancied 'dance' into a concrete reality, and demonstrates that it not only should but can over-ride personal anguish. In doing so, she summons up ideas that are more than narrowly aristocratic:

> *Dauncing* (bright Lady) then began to be,
> When the first seedes wherof the world did spring,
> The Fire, Ayre, Earth and Water did agree,
> By Loves perswasion, Natures mighty King,
> To leave their first disordred combating;
>   And in a daunce such measure to observe,
>   As all the world their motion should preserve.
>
> Loe this is Dauncings true nobilitie.
> Dauncing the child of Musick and of Love,
> Dauncing it selfe both love and harmony,
> Where all agree, and all in order move;
> Dauncing the Art that all Arts doe approve:
>   The faire Caracter of the worlds consent,
>   The heav'ns true figure, and th'earths ornament.[1]

Sir John Davies's long poem 'Orchestra Or a Poeme of Dauncing', printed in 1596, provides a gloss on the dance in Act V of *The Broken Heart*, linking it with a great Renaissance and classical tradition. Through the exercise of will, Calantha holds the court together in an order and harmony sanctioned and repeated by the seasons, the constellations, the tides, and the fruitful marriage of the elements. She defends a society threatened by chaos and monstrosity. Precisely because she does not break up her lines to weep, she vindicates Sparta's exacting code of reason, measure and self-control as something which can be exemplified by human beings, not merely by the books they write.

Structurally, the unviolated symmetry and closure of the dance in Ford's play answers all of those masques, shows, plays within the play and other entertainments which had disintegrated into confusion at the end of so many Elizabethan and Jacobean revenge tragedies. It gains its effect largely because of the way it contradicts an established theatrical tradition, becoming an affirmation rather

[1] Sir John Davies, 'Orchestra Or a Poeme of Dauncing', in *The Poems of Sir John Davies*, ed. Robert Krueger (Oxford, 1975), 94, 115.

than an agent of destruction.[1] The last change concluded, Calantha begins her reign 'with a first act of justice' (v.ii.67). She sentences Orgilus to death, reminds the company that the departed must have paid their debt to mortality one time or another, and announces that 'we'll suddenly prepare our coronation' (v.ii.93). This line seems to bring the tragedy to its end, on a note at once admirable and chilling. The 'masculine spirit' (v.ii.95) of Calantha has elicited from the awed members of the court a reaction which speaks for the theatre audience as well: a compound of wonder, humility, relief, and a certain discomfort. This woman who has just lost her father, her lover, and her friend seems, in her iron self-control, both more and less than human. The suspicion arises that, paradoxically, the high, rational ideals of Sparta can only be embodied by someone who is emotionally a monster.

Ford allows such an ending to flicker as a possibility, and then unexpectedly moves beyond it. It seems that Orgilus' execution is to take place not only within the time span of the play, but on stage. The blood-letting itself, detailed, protracted, and made more disturbing by the controlled hysteria of Bassanes' commentary, presents an image of violence *and* repose. This is an oxymoron which operates primarily on a visual level, but it is no less powerful for that. The whole play has worked to create a powerful sense of energies and passions repressed, bottled up within limits too narrow. The release of Orgilus' turbulent, pent-up blood is both ghastly and somehow gratifying: a 'pastime' as Bassanes terms it (v.ii.131) in deadly earnest, a game in which the will controls the body, an 'honourable infamy' (v.ii.123). As a stoic display, it is raw, crude, but effective. At its conclusion, the tragedy gestures deceptively once again at an ending:

> The coronation must require attendance;
> That past, my few days can be but one mourning.
>
> (v.ii.158–9)

[1] It is possible that Ford remembered Marston's use of a court dance in *The Malcontent*, some years earlier, to conduct the play towards a final social harmony.

Bassanes' valedictory lines sound final. And indeed there appears to be no plot material remaining, no expectations unfulfilled. Orgilus, Ithocles, Penthea and Amyclas are dead, Prophilus and Euphranea united, Bassanes reformed, and Calantha rules in Sparta. Whether or not she eventually accepts Nearchus as husband is a matter of no import. The woman who displayed such 'tokens/Of constancy' (v.iii.16–17), as Armostes puts it, in the last scene is clearly capable of governing alone.

Nothing prepares either the theatre audience or its surrogates on stage for another scene, one in which the play's title will be reinterpreted, Calantha's true nature revealed, and the ethos of Sparta made human. The queen's prayer before the altar at the beginning of this scene may well be a request for death, a request granted by the gods. Nevertheless, there is about her extinction the sense of a supreme triumph, a mastery of mind over body which alters, in retrospect, the way we regard Penthea's last will and testament, and her death by starvation, as it modifies the effect of Orgilus' suicide. Like Yeats's old man of Tara, who decided in his 101st year that his life had gone on long enough,

> Saw that the grave was deep, the coffin sound,
> Summoned the generations of his house,
> Lay in the coffin, stopped his breath and died,[1]

Calantha dies through a conscious and calculated movement of the mind. She does not need to starve herself out of existence, like Penthea, nor does she become in the slightest degree irrational. Her final disposition of people, her ordering of the succession and of Sparta's high offices are irreproachable. Unlike Orgilus, she does not even require the aid of a knife. She simply wills herself to stop living, and that will—whose strength has already been demonstrated in her continuation of the dance—performs what is required of it.

Like Ithocles, Orgilus and Penthea before her, Calantha arranges for music to express something she cannot easily say. A lyric relief from the rigours of the play's spare, aristocratic norm

[1] William Butler Yeats, 'In Tara's Halls', in *Collected Poems of W. B. Yeats* (London, 1961), 374.

of dramatic speech, the four songs of *The Broken Heart* release emotion to flow in freer and less restricted channels, without for an instant dissipating its intensity.[1] This is true even of the song Orgilus sings to bless the marriage of Prophilus and Euphranea, although it appears at a moment less ominous than the other three. For the dying Penthea, the desperate Ithocles of Act III, and Calantha at the end, music crystallizes emotion. It objectifies feelings which have become intolerable, an agony which these people have tried to repress as long as possible. But Calantha's song, written we are told by herself, has a quality all its own. Appropriately, for someone who has elected to become queen, bride, and corpse all in the same moment, it focuses upon the paradoxes of Time:

> Crowns may flourish and decay;
> Beauties shine, but fade away.
> Youth may revel, yet it must
> Lie down in a bed of dust.
> Earthly honors flow and waste;
> Time alone doth change and last.
> Sorrows mingled with contents prepare
>   Rest for care;
> Love only reigns in death, though art
> Can find no comfort for a broken heart.
>
>   (v.iii.85–94)

In a world of transience and mutability, 'Time alone doth change and last'. But Time, as both Crotolon and Penthea have observed earlier, has a 'daughter': 'truth is child of time' (iii.v.62, iv.iii.38). The riddles of the gods and the dark complexities of human feelings are alike impenetrable until 'events/Expound their truth' (iv.iii.36–7). No amount of interpretation or attempted analysis

---

[1] A number of scholars (S. P. Sherman, G. M. Carsaniga, Katherine Duncan-Jones) have felt that Ford was drawing attention in his prologue to parallels between Penthea's situation and that of Penelope Devereux, Sidney's Stella. The general indebtedness of *The Broken Heart* to Sidney's *Arcadia* has long been recognized. It may be more than coincidental that Ford's songs appear at an analogous point in the whole, and fulfil a very similar purpose, to those in the second half of Sidney's *Astrophil and Stella*.

on the part of other characters—or a theatre audience—can plumb them until the moment is ripe. Calantha's unpredictable funeral wedding, mingling sorrows with contents, is the last of the oxymorons in *The Broken Heart*. But it is different from its predecessors. In the tableau she stages at the end, the conflicting demands of an impersonal, public world and a private realm of the emotions, mind and body, stoicism and passion, are at last reconciled. In revealing the strength of her commitment to the murdered Ithocles, she fuses the contradictory terms which have bedevilled her society. Love still leads to death, but at least it is a death freely and intelligently chosen, and its legacy to others is order, not destruction. Unlike Penthea, Orgilus, or even Ithocles, Calantha in dying honours all the demands that life makes on people in Sparta. Unimaginable before it actually happens, the second catastrophe of *The Broken Heart* both exemplifies the aristocratic code at its best, and makes its peace with the heart's necessities. Far from being a structural fault, the last of the surprises Ford prepared for his theatre audience was an inspiration. It sets the seal on a dramatic technique—unorthodox, sometimes puzzling, but brilliant—which has operated throughout this play as a metaphor for the unknowability of fate.

V

Theatres, Gardens, and Garden-theatres

JOHN DIXON HUNT

A subtitle for my essay might be 'About Vauxhall and Ranelagh'. These London pleasure-gardens will serve as text, pretext and context; to write 'about' them is to explore a whole congeries of forms, themes and ideas of both garden and theatre. Variously and collaboratively these two artistic forms shaped each other's development during and after the Renaissance: many writers, for example, have noticed 'the close relationship which existed in seventeenth-century Italy between theatrical and garden architecture'.[1] This relationship was carried, like much else, into England and, like much else too, adapted to English art and society during the seventeenth and eighteenth centuries. Yet architectural form by itself is not my subject on this occasion; it is rather how the physical conditions of garden and/or theatre declare contemporary ideas of human nature and existence. Gardens and theatres (including stage scenery) search for their forms in a constantly changing attempt to articulate other, larger and less accessible aspects of life. By close attention to specific examples of garden and theatre such as Vauxhall and Ranelagh it is possible to give a sharper focus to those shadows thrown upon the walls of the cave (or, in theatrical terms, even *cavea*) of history.

Vauxhall and Ranelagh were the two most famous, because

[1] Georgina Masson, writing in *Queen Christina of Sweden. Documents and Studies*, ed. Magnus von Platen (*Analecta Reginensia*, I, Stockholm, 1966), 254. See below, in works cited on pp. 98 and 108, for other attention to this relationship.

Much of the research and the writing of a first draft of this essay were done while I was a member of the Institute for Advanced Study, Princeton, during the Spring Term, 1978. For their careful scrutiny of the draft at that time I am most grateful to Irving Lavin, Christoph Frommel and Lionello Puppi.

the most successful and long-lived, of London's pleasure-gardens.[1] But for two hundred years or more after the Restoration these two were simply the most prominent among many others, smaller, less ambitious (and so less able to survive by adapting to changing tastes and social customs), yet sharing with their major rivals features of garden and theatre which will occasionally be useful in illuminating Vauxhall and Ranelagh. Vauxhall was opened in 1661 as the New Spring Gardens: it comprised fountains, one large room, grass walks dividing the land into plots filled with fruit bushes, roses, shrubs as well as vegetables, and had arbours where visitors could eat snacks or, as Pepys often did, entertain some congenial companion. The form in which we know Vauxhall best was given it in the early 1730s by Jonathan Tyers, whose family retained the ownership until 1792 and thus oversaw the heyday of the gardens: now they were divided into larger sections by various cross-walks; there were pavilions, supper and music rooms, alcoves, an orchestra, and other exhibits dotted around the perimeter. By contrast, Ranelagh had a more restricted garden —opened in 1742 in the grounds of Lord Ranelagh's former house, its central feature was the huge, specially constructed Rotunda; but there were gravel walks, an octagonal lawn, a water-basin and a canal with its island and 'Chinese' or 'Venetian' temple.

These pleasure-gardens have been much studied for their social and anecdotal interest and for the personalities connected with them.[2] But other topics have consequently been neglected. How, for instance, did Vauxhall and Ranelagh combine their gardenesque and their theatrical functions? Why, indeed, should such gardens be considered as theatres at all? What precedents for such an alliance existed in England or on the Continent? Such enquiries

[1] See Warwick Wroth, *The London Pleasure Gardens of the Eighteenth Century* (London, 1896) and E. Beresford Chancellor, *The Pleasure Haunts of London* (London, Boston and New York, 1925).

[2] See, esp. James Granville Southworth, *Vauxhall Gardens. A Chapter in the Social History of England* (New York, 1941); Mollie Sands, *Invitation to Ranelagh 1742–1803* (London, 1946); W. S. Scott, *Green Retreats. The Story of Vauxhall Gardens 1661–1859* (London, 1955); Richard D. Altick, *The Shows of London* (Cambridge, Mass., 1978).

lead in their turn to questions about whether garden settings had special significance as stage designs. And then, finally, it is worth asking what light is thrown by these garden-theatres at Vauxhall and Ranelagh upon the contemporary development of the landscape garden; did it, too, have theatrical implications which we now miss? Some attempt to answer this cluster of related questions will, it is hoped, interest the theatre as well as the garden historian and direct the attention of the literary critic afresh to texts which invoke these garden-theatres.

Vauxhall, from its earliest years, was obviously associated with a strongly theatrical dimension of social life, which was given, under Tyers's management, a visible and formal aspect. This was not, however, the clearly theatrical character of its nineteenth-century existence, when it became one stop on the London circuit for miscellaneous entertainers for whom stages and auditoriums were erected.[1] The mid-eighteenth-century gardens rather took their theatrical aspect from various architectural features, closely connected (albeit in muddled fashion) with actual theatres.

First, there were the three curving pavilions around the central grove, familiar from bird's-eye views. These constructions were 'theatres' in that their apsidal shape echoed a standard feature of Renaissance garden architecture, itself indebted to many readings and misreadings of classical ruins including theatres like that of Marcellus in Rome as well as baths, libraries and nymphaeums. John Evelyn, for instance, remarked upon the 'theatre for pastimes', when he visited Carlo Fontana's strikingly scenographic climax to the gardens of the Villa Mondragone at Frascati.[2] Such apsidal elements were a basic device in Italian garden design from Bramante's early *exedra* in the Belvedere Courtyard at the Vatican, itself copied from the Temple of Fortuna Primigenia at Palestrina, which it is now recognized was indeed used for

[1] See Altick, *The Shows of London*, 250, 344, 360 and 373.
[2] *The Diary*, ed. E. S. de Beer (Oxford, 1955), II, 393. Mondragone is illustrated in C. L. Franck, *The Villas of Frascati* (1966). For some attempt to define 'theatre' in the context of a nearby Frascati villa, see Klaus Schwager, 'Kardinal Pietro Aldobrandinis Villa Di Belvedere in Frascati', *Römisches Jahrbuch für Kunstgeschichte*, 9–10 (1961–2), 379–82.

various ritual performances.[1] The shape of a concave wall, perhaps with niches, or even an alcove cut into the hillside, sometimes mounted by a series of steps, became a permanent feature of seventeenth- and eighteenth-century garden design in France and England. But this is also the place to recall that courtyards, such as the Belvedere or that between the Pitti Palace and the Boboli Gardens in Florence, became spaces for theatrical and other entertainments; gardens were designed with amphitheatres, the Boboli again, for representations. The Italian garden, in short, made an essential contribution to what Jean Jacquot and his colleagues at the Centre National de la Recherche Scientifique have called, following Corneille, *le lieu théâtral*.[2]

Vauxhall undoubtedly absorbed this basic, but distinctly theatrical, form for its first major garden buildings in the 1730s. The curving pavilions declared themselves as 'theatres' and cleared a space within their scope as an amphitheatre. (Later, when Ranelagh had set a fashion with its Rotunda—originally described as an amphitheatre,[3] Vauxhall established its indoor arenas in various buildings: a rotunda, picture room and supper room, all entered from one of the original curving pavilions.) These pavilions were themselves divided into innumerable niches, simply the adaptation to mass entertainment of garden alcoves, which derived ultimately from the classical *exedra* or conversation seats decorated with pictures that Cicero describes in his villa.[4] Such decorations were even adopted by Tyers at Vauxhall, where the

[1] For the Belvedere see J. S. Ackermann, 'The Belvedere as a Classical Villa', *J.W.C.I.*, XIV (1951), 70–91, and Hans Henrik Brummer, *The Statue Court in the Vatican Belvedere* (Stockholm, 1970); for Palestrina, the ancient Praeneste, see John Arthur Hanson, *Roman Theater-Temples* (Princeton, N.J., 1959), 33–6.

[2] For Belvedere, see note above; for Pitti Palace, see Roy Strong, *Splendour at Court* (1973). Of the volumes issued by the C.N.R.S. the most relevant here are *Le Lieu Théâtral à la Renaissance*, ed. Jean Jacquot, Elie Konigson and Marcel Oddon (Paris, 1964), esp. the essay by André Chastel, 'Cortile et Théâtre', and *Les Fêtes de la Renaissance*, ed. Jean Jacquot, 2 vols. (Paris, 1956 and 1960), through there is little attention to gardens specifically. See also A. M. Nagler, *Theatre Festivals of the Medici 1539 to 1637* (New Haven, 1964).

[3] *A Description of Ranelagh Rotunda and Gardens* (1762), 8. The rotunda at Vauxhall had a stage, boxes, gallery and a pit which could be used as an arena.

[4] *Epistulae Ad Familiares*, VII, 23.

booths were each supplied with a picture by Francis Hayman after his and Hogarth's designs.[1]

Now, such classical allusions—and we shall encounter more— are not of themselves likely to establish a specifically theatrical character. But the *exedra*, whether as intimate alcove or larger *frons scaenae*, had acquired an ambiguous status in garden design, and this Vauxhall manipulated with success. The scenographic garden at Mondragone, for example, was both stage—its statues and fountains viewed from the garden below—and auditorium or *cavea*—a rostrum from which to view the gardens. Less ostentatious *exedra* seats were both vantage points whence to watch other events and stages where visitors themselves were made to feel the constituted the garden dramas.[2] For the Italian garden that most influenced France and England was one where the visitor was no longer a passive spectator; he was led, instead, as Sir Henry Wotton declared in a famous passage, 'by severall *mountings* and *valings,* to various entertainements of his *sent,* and *sight*'[3]. The expectation of a fine garden, whatever the formal means by which the effects were achieved, was that it work upon its visitor, involving him often insidiously as a participant in its dramas, which were presented to him as he explored its spaces by a variety of statues, inscriptions and (above all) hydraulically-controlled automata.

It follows, I think, from these expectations of a fine garden that gardens also expressed some of the more complicated notions of the idea of *theatrum mundi*. Elizabethan audiences at the Globe Theatre had expected—the very scene they watched enforced this —to view a microcosm of the world. Gardens, too, were designed to include a conspectus of allusions. The words *theatre* and *garden*, indeed, were used interchangeably to mean a collection or compendium: as in John Parkinson's *Theatrum Botanicum, The Theatre*

---

[1] See Lawrence Gowing, 'Hogarth, Hayman, and the Vauxhall Decorations', *Burlington Magazine*, 95 (1953), 4–19.

[2] An English example is recorded in the Stoke Edith hangings: see Thomasina Beck, *Embroidered Gardens* (1979), 75.

[3] *Elements of Architecture* (1624), 109–10. For further commentary on this aspect of gardens see my '"Loose Nature" and the "Garden Square": The Gardenist Background for Marvell's Poetry,' *Approaches to Marvell*, ed. C. A. Patrides (1978).

of Plants, or an Universall and Complete Herball (1640) and Henry Peacham's *Minerva Britanna* (1612) which its subtitle explains as 'a Garden of Heroicall Devises, furnished and adorned with emblems and Impresas . . .' Such titles, as Erwin Panofsky remarked to Herbert Weisinger, intimate a 'world [that] becomes a grandiose spectacle, filled with floating images and a constantly changing scenery, rather than a structure clearly organized and intellectually penetrable'.[1] The promise of a whole world of items which the words and arts of theatre and garden held out was, as Panofsky suggests, not always redeemed in straightforward ways. If stage and garden dramatize the world, the world was also traditionally a theatre, and the concepts were mutually endorsing and complicating. The simplest idea of *theatrum mundi* is that we are placed as admiring spectators in the theatre of the world; but soon this slips into our being also actors, perhaps (as Plato implied) radically unsure of our true role in life's drama; from this it is another simple step into believing that 'the very *mythos* of the play of life is itself a falsehood'.[2] These shifting concepts were equally relevant to gardens as theatres—compendiums, that is, or stages where life's variety was made visible.

These ideas are rarely applied to garden design, despite the testimony of Henry Wotton and other amateurs. But it is evident that not only did seventeenth- and early eighteenth-century gardens promote the shifting perspectives of which Panofsky wrote but they were organized in order to ensure them. Vauxhall Gardens was a commercial exploitation of these garden traditions; if it catered largely to citizens with little experience of other, private gardens, its other clients from Pepys to Johnson certainly had that experience, and its very organization of visitors within

---

[1] Copies of Panofsky's correspondence with Weisinger are at the Institute for Advanced Study and I am grateful to Mrs Gerda Panofsky for drawing them to my attention. Some quotations are given in Herbert Weisinger, *The Agony and the Triumph* (East Lansing, Michigan, 1964), in the course of his essay on 'Theatrum Mundi: Illusion as Reality', 58–70.

[2] Besides Weisinger's essay (ibid.), see also Richard Bernheimer, 'Theatrum Mundi', *Art Bulletin*, 38 (1956), 225–47, Jean Jacquot, 'Le Théâtre du Monde de Shakespeare à Calderón', *Revue de littérature comparée*, 31 (1957), 341–72, and Anne Righter (Barton), *Shakespeare and the Idea of the Play* (1962).

the grounds subtly manipulated even the uninitiate into theatrical expectations.

Vauxhall and Ranelagh were designed to include various theatrical forms, like the curving pavilions, their niches and the rotunda amphitheatres. Furthermore the gardens were provided with many other items quite specifically associated with the theatre: there were the real vistas down the walks, assisted on the Italian Walk by a series of triumphal arches that accentuated the long prospect like wings; there were the illusionistic prospects, *trompe-l'oeil* scenes at the end of walks, like a painting of the ruins of Palmyra that closed the South Walk or the two arches of some Roman acqueduct at the end of the Cross Walk (these last made to seem real in an engraving after Canaletto). This repertoire of exotic backdrops was further augmented by various transparencies, sometimes actually hung in front of small stages: one of these depicted a Hermit pursuing his studies by the light of a fire and a brilliant moon, while another, immediately at the entrance to the gardens, represented an amphitheatre through which was visible a garden perspective terminated with a pedestal. This mingling of garden and theatre imagery—to the point where demarcations became blurred (Ranelagh's supper boxes *inside* the Rotunda opened at their rear into the gardens)—recalls many Renaissance theatrical events to which reference will be made later.

Confusions of art and reality, a staple feature alike of garden and theatre, were further pursued at Vauxhall in *tableaux* or kinematic illusions, like the famous cascade which Tyers created to rival Garrick's at Drury Lane. It displayed a water-mill, miller's house and a foaming waterfall, made of tin. Its attraction, attested by Goldsmith's Mrs Tibbs as by Burney's Evelina,[1] was the strong illusion of reality—the foam at the base of the cascade was especially admired—contrived out of the palpably unreal: the 'switching-on' of this mechanism was actually announced by a warning bell to give people time to convene from all parts of the garden. In 1783 the cascade was replaced by a representation of a

[1] *The Citizen of the World*, letter 71; *Evelina* (Oxford English Novels edn., 1968), 193 *et seq.*

'mountainous view covered with palm trees and circumscribed by a rainbow' (quoted Southworth, p. 50).

Yet if the cascade's replacement by a 'natural landscape' (ibid.) suggests that Vauxhall kept pace with contemporary taste, much more of its garden-theatre entertainments continued to rely heavily upon earlier episodes of garden history. In 1791, to honour the Prince of Wales's birthday, fireworks heralded the drawing up of a curtain at the end of the South Walk to discover

> a Gothic temple of a splendid figure, having an artificial fountain playing in its center, and beautifully decorated with twisted columns and various ornaments formed by transparencies and lamps. The columns and the chief part of the temple was a piece of curious machinery which kept in constant motion and formed a pleasing coup d'oeil.
>
> (Southworth, p. 60)

This grotto is a late (and cheap) version of those innumerable Italian mechanisms that entertained visitors like Evelyn at Pratolino and other gardens.[1] Well into the nineteenth century Vauxhall even put on *trompe-l'oeil* naumachia (see Southworth, pp. 60–61), yet another invocation of a Renaissance revival of classical entertainments, in pursuit of which the Pitti Palace courtyard was once flooded and which the lowest water terrace of the Villa Lante at Bagnaia wittily imitates in fountain sculpture. Some of the earliest entertainments in the New Spring Gardens were the hydraulic inventions of Sir Samuel Morland, who leased Vauxhall House after the Restoration; and according to Scott (p. 19) the name of the gardens derived from the water tricks or *giocchi d'acqua* which wetted unwary visitors; these devices had been an unfailing source of amusement to travellers in Italy from Montaigne to Evelyn.

To those who paid their entry fee to Vauxhall Gardens such

[1] For Evelyn at Pratolino, see *Diary*, II, 418–19. An interesting confusion of cave (or grotto) and *cavea* (or auditorium in a theatre) seems to have been made at least once during the Renaissance in documents on the Villa Lante—see Claudia Lazzaro-Bruno, 'The Villa Lante at Bagnaia', *Art Bulletin*, 59 (1977), 559 and note 36.

spectacles were offered as entertainment and by many visitors their earlier associations with gardens were unnoticed. Other features of Vauxhall, presented to its clients by way of entertainment, were adapted from garden vocabulary generally available in the eighteenth century, at least until the influence of 'Capability' Brown was felt. The most obvious items were the statues: the famous Roubiliac Handel[1] or the figure of Milton, seated on a rock in a listening posture in the area known as the 'Rural Downs'. At various times during the eighteenth century (the changes were simply commercial expedients to maintain the flow of visitors) the gardens were dotted with further items of a 'readable' nature—an obelisk with a Latin inscription, the paintings in the supper boxes (subjects were mostly images of play and recreation, apt for the site) and further emblems and paintings in the rotunda and its extension, the picture room. Classical images were frequently invoked—for the historical allegories painted by Hayman in 1760–61 and installed in the picture room, the casts of Diana, Apollo, Aurora (standing tiptoe on some 'mountains' at the end of the Grand Walk) and even a copy of the Apollo Belvedere. That Tyers counted upon the 'readability' of these images and considered a garden incomplete without a whole repertory of speaking pictures and statues is clear from the design of his own private gardens near Dorking. With their 'labyrinth of walks, some descending, some ascending: in some parts easy, smooth, and level; in others, rugged and uneven' they must have put their visitors to much exploration. But the gardens were famed for their 'moral sentences and admonitions', either inscribed on flags hanging 'at every turn' or decorating the Temple of Death (thoughtfully provided with a desk for reading and meditation) or issuing out of two real human skulls at the entrance to the Valley of the Shadow of Death. Deep in this gloomy valley was Tyers's *pièce de résistance*: an alcove in two compartments,

---

[1] Handel was presented in 'the stress and strain of composition' (Scott, 26). See also Terence Hodgkinson, *Handel at Vauxhall*, a booklet reprinted in 1969 from the *Victoria and Albert Museum Bulletin*, I (1965).

in one of which the unbeliever is represented dying in the
greatest distress and agony, crying—'Oh, whither am I going?'
... On one side, and above him, are his study of books, which
buoyed him up in his libertine course, such as Hobbes, Toland,
Tindal, Collins, Morgan, and others of the same stamp. In the
other compartment, is the good Christian, or believer, in his
dying moments, calm and serene ... the Bible open before him,
which, with several practical discourses upon it, and the sermons
of our most noted divines, such as Clarke, Tillotson, and others
of the kind, serve to make up his study.[1]

The whole representation was painted by Hayman, who had also
decorated the Vauxhall supper boxes. Tyers's organization of his
pleasure-gardens, while shrewdly not putting off his clients with
such strong moral injunctions, reveals him utilizing similar
garden imagery and effects.

Vauxhall's theatrical forms and scope throw into relief the
same, but generally neglected, aspect of English private gardens
between 1650 and 1750. There is space here only for brief examples in lieu of a proper survey. We have seen how Wotton
appreciated the theatrical excitements of an 'incomparable'
Italian garden and how Evelyn's visits to others elicited similar
responses. Visitors to the Villa D'Este at Tivoli often responded to
its series of events in language derived from the masque.[2] This
highly manipulative aspect of Italianate designs was translated into
French and English versions: the Earl of Arundel placed the
magnificent head of Jupiter given him by Sir Dudley Carleton 'in
his *utmost* garden', that is to say, in a distant part of his sculpture
garden besides the Thames, 'so opposite to the Gallery dores, *as
being open*, so soon as y^u enter into the front Garden y^u have the
head *in yor eie all the way*'.[3] Thus the visitor was drawn into the
excitements of discovery among the rest of the sculpture collection. By chance some mutilated fragments from Arundel's garden

[1] Quotations are from *The Vauxhall Papers* (1841), 51–3, which use contemporary descriptions.
[2] 'In the descent into the first garden shews itself the Colossus of Pegasus ...'
or 'riseth an Island cut in the shape of a ship', in Edmund Warcupp, *Italy in Its
Originall Glory, Ruine and Revivall* (1660), 309–11.
[3] Quoted D. E. L. Haynes, *The Arundel Marbles* (Oxford, 1975), 4, my italics.

were incorporated into another of the early pleasure-gardens, Cuper's (corrupted quickly to Cupid's) in Lambeth, where 'they received very ill usage from the Ignorance and Stupidity of those who know not their Value, and are still exposed to the open Air, and Folly of Passerby'.[1] But the history of these particular Arundel marbles nicely illuminates the absorption by the popular garden-theatres of ingredients from private gardens, themselves created in emulation of classical prototypes.

But as the visitor to Wotton's 'incomparable' garden or to Arundel's was led among the entertainments he would be forced to stop occasionally in front of grottoes, *exedras*, fountains and other 'theatres' to watch some extended spectacle. As the travel accounts of many Englishmen declare, these were the most attractive part of Italian garden art. The most sophisticated usually involved some display of automata, and as late a visitor as William Kent declared his appreciation of Pratolino's 'very fine groto's adorn'd with shells and petrified stone with pretty water works as Galatea coming out of her Grotto drawn by Dolfini'.[2] They contributed explicitly to the metamorphic world of Italian garden art, where one of the essential delights was the invitation to adjudicate continually the effects of art and nature. The seventeenth-century English and (early) French gardens readily copied such devices, as Evelyn's diary bears witness. Le Nôtre, the great French gardener to Louis XIV, disliked such frivolities, and they became less esteemed among the English. But the theatrical forms of Italian garden survived, even where their detailed exhibitions did not. So Le Nôtre's superb gardens at Vaux-le-Vicomte, for example, lead us down to the grand, double, water theatre, with river gods and their attendants as huge *tableaux* in niches, and on the way we see to left and right more intimate theatres let into

[1] John Aubrey, *Natural History and Antiquities of Surrey* (1719), 282 (the remark is by Aubrey's editor). Engravings of twenty-seven of Cuper's pieces were published in this *History*. On Arundel's garden, see Roy Strong, *The Renaissance Garden in England* (1979).

[2] The Bodleian Library, MS Rawl. D. 1162. Many drawings of these inventions at Pratolino were made by Giovanni Guerra in the sixteenth century and are now in the Albertina, Vienna; some are illustrated in two articles on Pratolino by Detlief Heikamp, *L'Oeil*, CLXXI (March, 1969), 16–27 and *L' Antiquità viva*, VIII (1969), 14–34.

the woods, in one of which Moliere's *Les Fâcheux* was performed
in 1661, with designs by Giacomo Torelli. Yet it did not need
actual representations to organize a garden's theatrical form and
ambience: two surviving gardens designed by John Evelyn at
Wotton and Albury in Surrey make this clear. The rear of the
house at Wotton gives upon a wide walk and circular pool backed
by an arcade, above which a terraced hillside rises; from these
terraces, which form the backdrop when viewed from the house,
the house and other gardens become the vista and the terraces a
rostrum for the spectator. At Albury, though the scale is larger,
the same change of role takes place as we move from the site of the
house, down into the valley and up the terraces. But in addition
the highest terrace is broken in the centre with a water theatre, like
those Evelyn admired in Frascati; from the middle of this, in its
turn, a tunnel disappears into the hillside in emulation of Posillipo
at Naples. Thus did Evelyn recreate, as it were, a memory
theatre which combined two souvenirs of his European journey.

The design of gardens, at least before 'Capability' Brown,
would continue to invoke structures which collected and composed some 'entertainments' for visitors. As the landscape movement grew, such events would be scattered amongst more
'natural' scenery, as happened at Stowe and Rousham: but the
Temple of Venus or of British Worthies at Stowe and the Vale of
Venus or Praeneste Terrace at Rousham all detain and focus for
visitors visual and verbal dramas, often engaging them as partici-
pants in understanding or even physically manoeuvring themselves
so that stage and auditorium might exchange places. One of the
earliest landscape designers to work at both Stowe and Rousham
was Charles Bridgeman, one of whose most distinctive 'signa-
tures' was the garden-theatre.[1] These probably owe their largest
debt to Le Nôtre's work, but the famous theatre at Claremont
derives directly from Serlio's codification of the Vatican Belvedere *exedra* in his *Cinque Libri d'Architettura*. But the main point
that Bridgemen's work enforces is that theatrical forms continued
to be a dominant feature of garden design at least until the mid-

[1] See Peter Willis, *Charles Bridgeman and the English Landscape Garden* (1978),
for some illustrations; but Willis does not discuss the theatres.

eighteenth century even where no evidence exists for actual dramatic representations. But that they continued to exercise some control over behaviour and thinking in gardens is clear. Bolingbroke's famous remark to Pope on the 'multiplied *scenes* of your little garden',[1] Pope's own delight in the entertainments of his garden and grotto, his iconographical representation (perhaps by Kent) in the cave or *cavea* of making, all testify to a theatrical dimension which we are inclined to neglect. Horace Walpole, who also acknowledged the dramas of moving through Pope's garden, was attentive elsewhere to these garden-theatres: at Stowe in 1770 he reported that

> A small Vauxhall was acted for us at the Grotto in the Elysian Fields, which was illuminated with lamps, as were the thicket and two little banks on the lake.[2]

His use of 'Vauxhall' as a generic noun (not by any means an isolated example) points to close relationships between garden, theatre and garden-theatre.

There is one magnificent visual example of a private garden, organized in a series of theatres, though doubtless Pope would not have appreciated its topiary. Balthasar Nebot's set of views of Hartwell House,[3] painted in the late 1730s, are of a late-seventeenth-century garden, remodelled perhaps by James Gibbs and Bridgeman. Nebot shows the immediate vicinity of the house laid out in various theatres which utilize pavilions and obelisks as termination points for perspectival scenes contrived in yew. Further, he shows the garden's owners and their friends responding, if undemonstrably, to the theatrical context, just as the very points of view he selects from which to paint declare the ambiguity of those theatres, which are sometimes stages and sometimes stations from which to observe the larger theatre of the new garden.

[1] *The Works of Henry St. John, Viscount Bolingbroke* (1754), III, 318, my italics.
[2] Walpole on Twickenham, I. W. U. Chase, *Horace Walpole: Gardenist* (Princeton, N. J., 1943), 28–9; on Stowe, *Horace Walpole's Correspondence*, ed. W. S. Lewis and others (New Haven, 1937 *et seq.*), X, 314.
[3] The paintings belong to Buckingham County Museum and are illustrated and briefly discussed by John Harris, *Country Life* (15 March 1979), 707–9.

The grounds of Hartwell House are made by Nebot to resemble seventeenth-century stage sets with garden scenery—they even suggest, though in fact this may not have been so, that the perspective tricks of stage scenery (whereby, as Serlio put it, 'a man in a small place may see . . . a thousand fayre things') have been rendered in yew. Gardens like these at Hartwell figured often in stage designs. One can only conclude that the two arts of perspective theatre scenery and garden design, first flourishing together in the Cinquecento, sustained and mutually inspired each other's endeavours then and later. Gardens not only incorporated theatres, but came to be planned *in toto* as theatres; while gardens featured prominently as dramatic locations in intermezzi, operas and plays.[1] Indeed, the exchanges between the arts were carried on occasions to subtle extremes: an opera performed in the Barberini Palace in 1656 had a row of fountains across the proscenium opening for which real water was piped from the gardens, while painted gardens appeared on the curtain.[2] A theatre constructed at the Buen Retiro Palace in Madrid in 1640 had a rear wall which parted to show real gardens beyond the illusionist ones.[3] We have already seen how Vauxhall Gardens continued to mix real and illusionary scenery, while a rival pleasure-garden, the Apollo, painted the end of its spacious indoor room with a landscape 'which concealed the orchestra from the public view' and presumably aided the illusion that the music came from out-of-doors.[4]

The parallel and sometimes joint endeavours of garden and

---

[1] The Villa Garzoni, at Collodi, near Lucca, both has a small theatre in the grounds and as a whole seems constructed like a steeply-sloping auditorium; there were many other examples, illustrated in such books as G. B. Falda, *Li Giardini di Roma* (1683). For some examples of gardens as stage settings, see Per Bjurström, *Giacomo Torelli and Baroque Stage Design* (Stockholm, 1961).

[2] Per Bjurström, *Feast and Theatre in Queen Christina's Rome* (Stockholm, 1966), 23 and plate 22. Aaron Hill's production of Handel's *Rinaldo* in 1711 showed a cascade with real water: *The Eighteenth-Century English Stage*, ed. Kenneth Richards and Peter Thomson (1972), 172–3.

[3] More details are given in my 'Marvell, Nun Appleton and the Buen Retiro', forthcoming in *Philological Quarterly*.

[4] There is a charming watercolour of this in John Fillinham's scrapbook, *The Public Gardens of London*, in the Guildhall Library.

theatre design introduce other considerations of more importance to the English literary historian. Granted that gardens occurred often as settings (by the later seventeenth century they were standard equipment for London theatres[1]) and granted that scenery in theatres and Italian-derived garden art were still new and exciting developments, did gardens have any special significance in dramatic representations? Did such scenery have its own visual codes or language upon which the verbal text depended?[2] Undoubtedly it did, though the sheer incidence of garden settings inevitably meant they were sometimes used in a token, unstrenuous fashion. But from the masques of Inigo Jones (a prime witness, since he knew Italian stage and garden art), through some Restoration plays, to *Arsinoë*, the special significance of gardens as dramatic setting is clearly, if variously, announced.

In Jones's masque designs gardens play two roles.[3] They may be the locale of ideal states, either political ('the beautiful garden of the Britanides', *Luminalia*) or seasonal ('spacious garden with walks, parterras, close arbours and cypress trees . . . all which figureth the spring', *Florimène*). This was, of course, a traditional significance of the garden, as in the Fount of Vertue and the Garden of Plenty depicted on the triumphal arches which greeted James I's entry into London. Yet equally traditional was the garden as trap and deceit, often associated with Circe, whose garden appeared in *Tempe Restored* as it had in earlier, Continental entertainments like the *Balet comique de la Royne* of 1581. Above all, gardens were uncertain territory, partly because of this double role they enjoyed. We must recognize the essential, exciting insecurity of a spectator's confrontation with a garden at an actual villa as in the masquing hall. The developments of Italian garden art that emphasized surprises and metamorphic play lent their

[1] Peter Holland, *The ornament of action. Text and performance in restoration comedy* (Cambridge, 1979), 36.

[2] A most valuable discussion of the semiotics of scenery, to which I am indebted, is contained in Peter Holland's study, mentioned in the previous note.

[3] All references in the following discussion are to Stephen Orgel and Roy Strong, *Inigo Jones. The Theatre of the Stuart Court*, 2 vols. (London, Berkeley and Los Angeles, 1973).

authority to all such dramatic ambiguities as well as contributing much more of their imagery than has been allowed. The opening rocks which disclosed Oberon's palace in 1611 recreate theatrically our experience of walking towards Buontalenti's grotto in the Boboli Gardens, where the distant sight of an architectural feature changes into a recognition of 'natural' stonework which finally, inside, completely surrounds us. Jones's mechanism simply reversed the experience.[1]

The scene from *Oberon* is typical of the masque's thematic and technical reliance upon transformation. In this, too, garden experience played an important part, for its essence was movement, often a carefully prepared sequence of events and discoveries, as the spectator was led onwards. The verbal texts of masques often emphasized this garden quality even in their descriptions of the static back-shutter designs; though Jones's design for 'A Garden and a Princely Villa' (II, plate 281) manages to convey a fine sense of our having arrived at the top of a flight of steps which lead into the excitements of a new garden. In *Lord Hay's Masque* we are told of 'two ascents', which as in any steeply terraced site force choices upon the visitor, 'that on the right leading to the bower of Flora, the other to the house of Night' (I, 116). *Tempe Restored* has a palace 'seated on side of a fruitful hill . . . with an open terrace before it and a great stair of return descending into the lower grounds' (II, 480). Sometimes the invocation of this garden movement is economical—*Luminalia*'s 'further part of the garden opened' (II, 708); but sometimes, as in *Coelum Britannicum*, much more elaborate:

> the scene again is varied into a new and pleasant prospect clean differing from all the other, the nearest part showing a delicious garden with several walks and parterr as set round with low trees, and on the sides against these walls were fountains and grots, and in the furthest part a palace from whence went high walks upon arches, and above them open terraces planted with

[1] Such garden debts (and see also the quotation from *Lord Hay's Masque* below) give some support to the theory that Jones was in Italy before his visit there with Arundel in 1613–14; see Orgel and Strong, I, 20 and note 24.

cypress trees, and all this together was composed of such orna-
ments as might express a princely villa.[1]

Such passages both work to ensure that the scene is 'read' correctly
and depend upon a knowledgeable response. Most other references
to gardens emphasize how much the new dramaturgy of the
masque, as Stephen Orgel and Roy Strong have explained it, also
constituted a garden's drama—'annihilating the barrier between
the ideal and the real' and requiring the active participation of the
audience whose 'wit and understanding made the miracles and
metamorphoses possible' (I, 1 and 13).

Wit and understanding could hardly be counted upon to the
same extent in the Restoration theatre; nor were the technical
resources as sophisticated. But audiences were probably expected
to 'read' garden settings as part of a comedy's full meaning. No
longer, of course, were these villas and princely gardens, but
public ones like Mulberry and Vauxhall (still known as New
Spring Gardens); however, what an audience expected of
experiences in them seems to have differed very little. It is their
dramatic ambiguity that is invoked and involved in the plays:
places of pastoral perfection, accentuated by their 'gardenhood' (as
Walpole called it in 1769 when he thought it threatened), where
Valentine and Christine may plight their troth at the end of
Love in a Wood; but also places of intrigue, duplicity, play and
consequent confusions.

The Mulberry Garden uses both expectations. The eponymous
setting authorizes the pastoral heroics of Forecast's children as well
as libertine intrigue generally throughout the play. But two scenes
are actually set there. In one (I. iii) the country girls, Olivia and
Victoria Everyoung, prefer its intricate diversions to the 'long
walk at home' and enjoy rather innocently its amorous excitements ('the air of this place is a great softener of men's hearts').

[1] Orgel and Strong reject Simpson and Bell's identification of this design
(Orgel and Strong, plate 252) because it contains only one fountain, whereas
their suggestion (plate 281) honours the text's call for fountains and grottoes in
the plural. However, it seems clear that a knowledgeable gardenist would
register opportunities for fountains and grottoes in the rear pavilion of plate
252.

In another (iv.i) it is the intrigues and play that dominate; those gallants like Estridge and Modish who like to work the gardens are out-manoeuvred by Olivia and Victoria in conjunction with Wildish, who was taken there by the other two men to see if they could make him fall in love. In the setting of two adjacent arbours the hidden and masked girls are the audience of a double bill— Wildish's charade with the other two men and theirs with him. But the encounters of the gardens (Snappum claiming his locket) foil the gallants' performance and when they seek to ease their discomposure by turning to the neighbouring ladies in masks Olivia and Victoria reveal themselves. The garden-theatre rewards those who will not spend too long in disguise and the rather extreme revenge that Modish and Estridge take upon Wildish, who marries Olivia, is to lure to the Mulberry Garden a widow for whom Wildish was arranging a match, kidnap her and marry her to Estridge. Thus do garden intrigues issue for better and for worse in real rather than feigned relationships.

Other comedies manage to mediate between the two garden ambiences more subtly than Sedley, even making this the mainspring of an action. Lady Brute in *The Provoked Wife* is quite certain that '[New] Spring Garden' is the ideal location for her plot with Bellinda and she associates it with both 'surprise . . . the most agreeable thing in the world' and doing a 'good turn' (iii.iii). In *She Would If She Could* the Mulberry Garden and the New Spring Garden are where the libertines exercise their skills, but are out-manoeuvred by Ariana and Gatty, who thereby affirm the pastoral potential of such places. The libertines fall, as Peter Holland has noted[1] and as the treacherous world of gardens has always contrived; but their fall is in part and a little uneasily redeemed by those who play the gardens less gratuitously: indeed, as Courtall tells Freeman at the very start of ii.i, 'the fresh air' of the Mulberry Garden does expel the vapours of wine drunk elsewhere. The two scenes that Etherege sets in the Garden involve the audience's recognition not only of its contemporary significance (acknowledging at once Ariana's 'you seldom row to Fox Hall without some such plot against the city' (iv.ii)), but of their

[1] *Op. cit.*, 53.

potential as meaningful, even symbolic, settings. The stage designs may have been recognizable and 'realistic',[1] but there were aspects of the actual gardens which the stage could not reproduce: namely, criss-cross walks, spatial deceits and discoveries and the opportunities afforded to schemers to make topography work on their behalf. Yet II.ii clearly anticipates an audience's comprehension of how Ariana and Getty, masked, exploit the garden walks (*The Women go out, and go about behind the scenes*) to corner Courtall and Freeman even while making the men believe the opposite has happened (*Enter the Women, and after 'em Courtall at the lower door, and Freeman at the upper on the contrary side*). The stage directions simply invoke theatre geography which the audience must read as that of gardens.

As the gallants admit to each other as that scene gets under way, such garden encounters are always problematic ('I have been so often baulked with these vizard-masks'). Dramatists seem to use the pleasure-gardens as settings which register and promote discovery, disconcertion and confusion: the New Spring Garden of *She Would If She Could* (IV.ii) and the end of IV.iv of *The Provoked Wife*, also set there. But Vanbrugh illustrates how the fluid, if not problematical, roles of actor and audience in the garden-theatres could also serve a playwright's turn. Lady Fancyfull and her maid use an arbour in New Spring Garden from which to watch the others, who are themselves actors (Lady Brute and Bellinda) and audience (Constant and Heartfree), the deceiving and the duped, until Sir John's drunken intrusion upon the scene forces a reorganization of roles. Bellinda and Heartfree go off to pry into the 'secrets of the Garden', released as innocent spectators, while Lady Brute and Constant rehearse an old act. Illusion, discovery, reaction and realignment are the staple of Restoration dramatic action; but this theatrical dimension of life is thrown into strong relief by scenes set in gardens which endorse and actively encourage such sequences.

Thomas Clayton's opera, *Arsinöe, Queen of Cyprus*, first performed at the Theatre Royal, Drury Lane, in 1705, had garden sets designed by Sir James Thornhill which have exercised theatre historians for the light they throw upon stage conditions at the

[1] Ibid., 29 and 52.

time. But the significance of the settings has been ignored; indeed, one historian states that a design's subject 'has little to do with this opera'.[1] Peter Motteux's libretto, published in 1707, does however yield some evidence that the gardens, *de rigueur* perhaps in fine productions, signalled some of the meanings we have already discovered in Restoration comedy and Jones's masques. With *Arsinöe* we are back with a princely villa, but its message continues to be both the heroic, ideal paradise of love and the stage of love's confusions and despair. Thornhill's well-known sketch for the first scene—clipped hedges and arbours as wings, steps descending from the terrace of the stage into an illusionary parterre beyond, replete with fountains and *exedra*—is the setting for the Queen's slumbers and Ormondo's astonished discovery of her ('what heavenly Fair'). His servant, stumbling around in the darkness, heralds the confusions that follow as Ormondo prevents the murder of Arsinöe, pursues the attacker and leaves the Queen to flee in fright from the garden. Gardens recur twice in the opera, reminders of an idyllic world of sleeping beauty and love at first sight; but the set of II.i is a *Great Hall looking into a Garden*—affairs of state, resulting in Ormondo's fight with Feraspe, have pushed that world away into a distant prospect. Act II, scene viii brings the action outside once more (*Arsinöe alone. A Garden*); but it is her warring passions that she sings of and the garden's unstable paradise changes into despair and death as Ormondo is finally led off to prison.

It would be indeed surprising if the rise and progress of garden art in Italy, France and England, unlike anything seen there before, did not have profound implications for other arts and society. As always with the translation of ideas from the Continent, England's response and contribution were both delayed and consequently liable to be more eclectic. Vauxhall and Ranelagh in the eighteenth century illustrate this clearly. Jonathan Tyers's management of the former gave the theatrical potential of the Restoration pleasure-gardens shapes and opportunities drawn from a long history of garden and theatre. Significantly he democratized garden art, at a

[1] *The Eighteenth-Century English Stage* (see note 2, p. 108), 187. The Thornhill sets are also discussed by Richard Southern, *Changeable Scenery* (1952), 177–8.

time when it was still largely a rich man's pastime, and he maintained its links with theatre at a time when 'Capability' Brown's
designs were eliminating not only 'readability' from a landscape
but various theatrical forms and opportunities as well. And in this
connection it is worth noting that reactions to Brown's style,
whether William Chambers', the picturesque proponents' or
Humphry Repton's, all put these elements back into the landscape.

It is this ineluctable theatricality of Vauxhall and Ranelagh that
was so fascinating at the time and is interesting now. That these
gardens maintained close connections with the legitimate theatre
and benefited from an exchange of personnel is not, however, any
satisfactory explanation of the phenomenon.[1] There was in
increasingly larger sections of society (a fact upon which foreigners
remarked[2]) a taste for theatricality which discovered at places like
Vauxhall and Ranelagh increased scope for both fantasy and role
playing. These garden-theatres readily accommodated the *fête
champêtre* and the masquerade, both of which were naturalized in
England in the eighteenth century. The essence of masquerade, of
course, was the chance to disguise one's everyday self and play
with and in new, temporary roles; these in their turn, as Boswell
remarked, required 'a great flow of Spirits and a Readiness at
Repartee'.[3] If one did not know one's lines, they had to be im-
provised. This connects the vogue for masquerade, I think, with
the conversation piece: both derived from the *fête champêtre*, both
concern the art of living with people in society, with all the role
playing that involves,[4] and both made theatres out of their loca-

---

[1] Discussed in part by Sands and Altick (see note 2, p. 96). Vauxhall's famous
'Ridotto al fresco' takes its name from a word meaning resort, haunt, shelter and
so foyer of a theatre.

[2] Aileen Ribeiro, 'The Exotic Diversion. The Dress worn at masquerades in
eighteenth-century London', *Connoisseur*, 197 (1978), 7.

[3] Quoted, ibid., 7.

[4] On conversation pictures see the excellent discussion by Ronald Paulson,
Emblem and Expression (1975), 121–36. That the diversions of the pleasure-
gardens were compared with *fêtes champêtres* is clear from an engraving entitled
'The citizens fête champêtre' in a grangerized copy of *A Sunday Ramble*, which
chronicles visits to some gardens, in the Bromhead Library, Senate House,
University of London. On this theme generally, see Elizabeth Burns, *Theatricality* (1972).

tions at Ranelagh or some country house. For the masquerade may have started in such arenas as the Haymarket Opera House, organized by the Swiss Heidegger (Master of Revels to George II), pleasure-gardens during the summer months and, during the winter, Carlisle House in Soho Square (though it is interesting that even this indoor site was given distinctly gardenesque imagery with a grotto, elegant walks and trees[1]); but the masquerade's theatricality quickly left precise arenas and permeated the whole town. Pope's *Dunciad* gives 'Stage and Town' interchangeable status and the last chapter of *Peri Bathous* ironically anticipates the whole city becoming one vast theatre. Max Byrd reminds us, too, that the theatre is at the heart of London in James Thomson's *Winter* ('The Comic Muse/Holds to the world a picture of itself').[2]

Reactions to these developments, as in Pope's case, were mixed. I discount simple complaints of immorality; especially before Tyers's management, Vauxhall had a very *louche* reputation, as Pope's obscene interpretation of his own lines on Stowe makes clear in *A Master Key to Popery*.[3] But Tyers was at pains to clean up the image of Vauxhall, and the London magistrates as well worked to make such places safer and more decent. The complaints, nevertheless, continued and were, I suspect, unconscious or covert protests at the whole spread of theatricality itself. At its most extreme this allowed a Captain Watson to attend a masquerade as Adam in 'an unavoidable indelicacy of dress' or Elizabeth Chudleigh to appear at Ranelagh in 1749 as Iphigenia ready for the sacrifice, her dress or undress provoking Mrs Montagu to remark that the 'high priest might easily inspect the entrails of the victim'.[4]

Lydia in *Humphrey Clinker* conducts herself in a more seemly fashion, but Matthew Bramble's irascible view of Vauxhall is an

[1] On Carlisle House see article by Aileen Ribeiro (*op. cit.*), 4.

[2] *Dunciad*, l l. 108; *Winter*, ll. 650–51 (*The Seasons*, ed. James Sambrook, Oxford, 1972). Max Byrd, *London Transformed. Images of the City in the Eighteenth Century* (New Haven, 1978), 63.

[3] He cites 'Parts answ'ring Parts, shall slide into a whole' and comments 'As if his Ldsps fine Gardens were to be just such another Scene of Lewdness as Cupids Gardens or Faux-hall' (the Twickenham edn. of Pope's poetry, III. ii. 183).

[4] See article by Aileen Ribeiro (*op. cit.*), 11.

oblique commentary upon the stagey intrigue of his niece, who is not surprisingly delighted by the gardens.[1] The novel ends with the conventional but scarcely casual analogy of *theatrum mundi*: 'The comedy is near a close; and the curtain is ready to drop'. Yet throughout Smollett explores human playfulness and attitudes towards role playing, which are aptly focused during the visit to Vauxhall early in the novel. Lydia's enthusiasm stresses the complete range of diversions and people—the very microcosm which we have seen was expected of garden and theatre; she writes breathlessly of 'the variety of beauties . . . wonderful assemblage of the most picturesque and striking objects', not forgetting Vauxhall's approximation of the music of the spheres. Even those who resented or were sceptical of Vauxhall and the widespread theatricality (Mat Bramble's complaints are a grumbling reversal of his niece's) noted this completeness of life, like Fielding's 'here, in one confusion hurl'd,/Seem all the nations of the world'. *Concordia discors* evidently found fresh fields to exploit at Ranelagh, where in 1749 an anonymous versifier allowed as how

> Here the whole world in Miniature we see,
> This scheme makes even Contraries agree.[2]

So the gardens played the world and the world, as Pope obsessively charted, played at theatre. Hogarth, who satirized these developments in his 1724 engraving, *Masquerades and Operas or the Taste of the Town*, moved in his paintings from actual theatre scenes of Gay's *The Beggar's Opera* to subjects where private theatricals alert one to the ambiguous status of actor and audience and finally to the theatre of life itself and the roles played there by harlot, rake and apprentice. Fielding, similarly, deserted the theatre for the novel without leaving the stage. For an artist's resources and insights were undoubtedly extended by the current theatricality. Vauxhall and Ranelagh may have been the 'Two

---

[1] Relevant passages in the Penguin text of the novel are pp. 120–21 for Mat's reactions, 123–5 for Lydia's and 388 for the *theatrum mundi* reference.

[2] Fielding's verses are quoted by Aileen Ribeiro, 3, and the others are taken from an engraving of Ranelagh in the Guildhall Library.

Grand Seminaries of Luxury' that a 1769 edition of Defoe's *Tour* announced them as being,[1] but their curriculum was more extensive and more absorbing. Pope himself, however much he disliked the raging theatrical fever of the metropolis, always viewed it with mixed feelings, while his Horatian or Twickenham poems depend for their subtlety upon the dramatization of their poet and his setting. The eighteenth century sees a fresh potency accruing to the conventional metaphors by which such heroines as Evelina are introduced 'upon the great and busy stage of life'. Evelina's history is itself a chronicle of her own education in the complex human arena of role playing, and her visit to Vauxhall a key scene in that drama.

Places like Vauxhall, with their contrived rurality and pastoral theatres, were not popular simply because, as one historian has claimed, 'the Englishman has ever had a genuine love for the country' (Scott, p. 11). Even Sir Roger de Coverly (*Spectator*, 383) appreciated the contrivance, the pastoral art of Vauxhall. These garden-theatres expressed and encouraged a theatricality which eighteenth-century society and its arts adopted with enthusiasm and insight. Boswell was often at Vauxhall himself, as Rowlandson's famous watercolour testifies, and he is no mean witness to the art of playing various parts in life; so we should pay him special attention when he tells us that Vauxhall 'is peculiarly adapted to the taste of the English nation'.[2]

---

[1] *A Tour . . . of Great Britain* (7th edn., 1769), II, 172.
[2] *Life of Johnson* (Oxford Standard Authors Edn., 1961), 959. Max Byrd (*op. cit.*) has a brief but illuminating discussion of Boswell's playing with new identities (p. 65).

Shakespeare in Leigh Hunt's Theatre Criticism

STANLEY WELLS

Leigh Hunt was only twenty years old when, in May 1805, his brother John started a paper called *The News* and asked him to be its theatre critic. He wrote regularly for it until the end of 1807. This makes him the first of our distinguished theatre critics to have engaged in regular criticism of performances shortly after they were given. In his *Autobiography* (1858) he writes interestingly about the state of theatre criticism at the time.[1] It was customary 'for editors of papers to be intimate with actors and dramatists'. The result was a good deal of corruption.

> Puffing and plenty of tickets were . . . the system of the day. It was an interchange of amenities over the dinner-table; a flattery of power on the one side, and puns on the other; and what the public took for a criticism on a play was a draft upon the box-office, or reminiscences of last Thursday's salmon and lobster-sauce. The custom was, to write as short and as favourable a paragraph on the new piece as could be; to say that Bannister was 'excellent' and Mrs Jordan 'charming'; to notice the 'crowded house' or invent it, if necessary; and to conclude by observing that 'the whole went off with *éclat*'.

The Hunt brothers decided that 'independence in theatrical criticism would be a great novelty. We announced it, and nobody believed us; we stuck to it, and the town believed everything we said.' Writing many years later, Hunt clearly finds something

---

[1] *The Autobiography of Leigh Hunt*, World's Classics edn. (1928). Leigh Hunt's theatre criticism is quoted from *Critical Essays on the Performers of the London Theatres* (1808), *Dramatic Essays by Leigh Hunt*, eds. William Archer and Robert W. Lowe (1894), and *Leigh Hunt's Dramatic Criticism 1808–1831*, eds. L. C. and C. W. Houtchens (New York, 1949). References to these volumes in this essay identify them respectively as *Performers*, Archer, and Houtchens.

pompous about his younger self: 'To know an actor personally appeared to me a vice not to be thought of; and I would as lief have taken poison as accepted a ticket from the theatres.' He admits to feeling shame at his own presumption in undertaking so responsible a task while still so young and inexperienced, though he seems more concerned with the problems that he had found in criticizing new plays than with his treatment of revivals of the classics. And he admits that he does not feel these early criticisms

> had no merit at all. They showed an acquaintance with the style of Voltaire, Johnson, and others; were not unagreeably sprinkled with quotation; and, above all, were written with more care and attention than was customary with newspapers at that time. The pains I took to round a period with nothing in it, or to invent a simile that should appear offhand, would have done honour to better stuff.[1]

In other words, he was writing literary essays, and may at times have been tempted to sacrifice truth to effect.

Early in 1808, Hunt published a volume called *Critical Essays on the Performers of the London Theatres*, made up of many essays on individual performers, written not as notices of separate performances, but as retrospective studies based on his own theatregoing. The volume includes a long Appendix, reprinting extracts from the criticisms first printed in *The News*. It is one of the main sources (other than the original newspapers) for a study of Hunt's theatre criticism. Another is *Dramatic Essays by Leigh Hunt*, edited by William Archer and Robert Lowe, published in 1894 and now difficult to come by. It includes an excellent introduction by Archer, and a selection of the essays from *The News*.

In January 1808 the Hunt brothers launched a new periodical, *The Examiner*, which appeared every Sunday. Again Leigh Hunt undertook the theatre criticism. Archer feels that he did so in a generally less censorious frame of mind than he had displayed in *The News*, but Hunt himself wrote that 'The spirit of the criticism on the theatres continued the same as it had been in the *News*.'[2]

---

[1] *Autobiography*, 190–2, 197.
[2] Ibid., 214.

Certainly Hunt did not abstain from making personal remarks about leading actors. Praising Kemble for his good taste in keeping Shakespeare before the public, he wrote,

> The other Managers of the present day have so little taste, with the exception of Sheridan who cares for no taste but that of port, that were it not for Mr Kemble's exertions the tragedies of our glorious bard would almost be in danger of dismissal from the stage;

and Mrs Faucit cannot have been pleased to be told, in relation to her performance as Volumnia, that

> A Roman matron did not think it essential to her dignity to step about with her head thrown half a yard back, as if she had a contempt for her own chin.[1]

Hunt made enemies by his outspokenness, and one of his weekly essays is largely given over to a defence of himself against charges of over-severity. At least this quality had the merit of increasing respect for him in those whom he praised. There is evidence for this in the biography of the famous comic actor, Charles Mathews, written by his wife, who says that 'the success' of one of Mathews's performances in 1808 'was recorded by the greatest dramatic critic of that day, Mr Leigh Hunt, whose judgment was universally sought and received as infallible by all actors and lovers of the drama'.[2] Hunt's notices in *The Examiner* give the impression of having been written with time to spare. They are little essays, including literary criticism as well as analyses of performances. Hunt went on writing for *The Examiner* until it ceased publication in 1821, though with a gap of two years spent in prison because of his excessive outspokenness on non-theatrical matters, which resulted in legal action against him for libelling the Prince Regent. A selection of the criticisms written during these years is printed in *Leigh Hunt's Dramatic Criticism 1808–1831* (1949),

[1] Houtchens, 38, 225.
[2] Mrs Anne Mathews, *Memoirs of Charles Mathews, Comedian*, quoted in Archer, xxx, note 1.

edited by L. C. and C. W. Houtchens, the most scholarly edition of any of our theatre critics.

In 1830, impelled by poverty, Leigh Hunt began to write, almost single-handed, a daily newspaper of four folio pages called *The Tatler*, which lasted until 1832 and included a high proportion of theatre criticism. Hunt himself considered that he never wrote 'theatricals so well, as in the pages of this most unremunerating speculation'.[1] Understandably, these notices are usually briefer than those written for the weekly *Examiner*. They sometimes include comment on the plays performed, but consist mainly of discussion of the performances of the principal actors. A few are reprinted in the Houtchens volume; a larger selection forms the second part of the Archer and Lowe collection.

Leigh Hunt's theatre criticism extends, then, over a quarter of a century. In discussing its relevance to Shakespeare I shall treat it as a single body of work, while drawing attention to chronological considerations when it seems desirable to do so. Hunt was, throughout his life, an omnivorous reader; and this fact shows in much of his writing. He refers often to Dr Johnson's Shakespeare criticism, but most of his references end in disagreement. Hunt defends Shakespeare's ending for *King Lear* against Johnson's criticism of it; he finds that Johnson's remarks on *King John* are 'in the usual spirit of the Doctor's criticism, consisting of assertions very well founded, but careless of all proof'; similarly, quoting Johnson on *Julius Caesar*, he writes, 'this is a sorry piece of criticism: it is, at best, like most of his criticisms, only so much gratuitous opinion without analysis, without argument'; he even goes so far as to assert that it is a 'betrayal of his absolute unfitness for poetical criticism, at least with regard to the works of a higher order'; and he praises Hazlitt's *Characters of Shakespear's Plays* by saying that 'it must inevitably supersede the dogmatic and half-informed criticisms of Johnson'.[2] In reacting against Johnson, Hunt reveals himself as a child of his time, at one with the other, greater proponents of Romanticism with whom he had many associations.

[1] *Autobiography*, 500.
[2] Houtchens: on *Lear*, 16–17; *King John*, 38; *Julius Caesar*, 65; Hazlitt, 289.

Of the essay in which Hunt defends Shakespeare's decision to show the death of King Lear, L.C. and C. W. Houtchens write,

> This review is historically significant in romantic Shakespeare criticism. It appeared in the same spring [of 1808] that Schlegel was lecturing on Shakespeare in Vienna, and Coleridge on Shakespeare at the Royal Institution. Hunt's sympathy with the romantic point of view is apparent here in his attack on Dr Johnson and the neo-classical objection to Shakespeare's disregard of poetic justice. . . . Through this review and certain of his later articles on the drama, Hunt added impetus to the English romantic movement by his adoption of romantic criteria . . .[1]

The extent of Coleridge's indebtedness to Schlegel in his Shakespeare criticism is still a matter for debate, though it seems now to be agreed that it was considerable but unacknowledged. Hunt expresses his admiration for Schlegel in his review of Hazlitt's *Characters of Shakespear's Plays*, where he describes Schlegel as the 'critic, who, with the exception of a few scattered criticisms from Mr Lamb, had hitherto been the only writer who seemed truly to *understand* as well as feel him [Shakespeare]'. Hunt praised Hazlitt as the first Englishman to have done 'justice to Shakspeare's characters in general'.[2] He had little to say about Coleridge, whose criticism he seems to have underrated, although he attended at least one of Coleridge's Shakespeare lectures of 1811.

Anyhow, members of the literary circles of the Romantic period held so many ideas in common that it is often impossible to determine who thought of what first. It is perhaps more important to observe the community of ideas and their distinctive features. It seems significant that Hunt praised Hazlitt as the first in England to show thorough appreciation of Shakespeare's *characters*. Hunt shared the characteristic Romantic concern with individuality, as is clear from his strong emphasis upon the actor's realization of idiosyncratic character traits. This is reflected partly in the kinds of

[1] Ibid., 295.
[2] Ibid., 291, 173.

acting that he admired. He has a number of interesting discussions of tragic acting, expressing admiration for what he regarded as a 'natural' style, and dislike of the evidently artificial. For example, on his first visit to the theatre after his imprisonment, in 1815, he saw for the first time Edmund Kean, who had had a meteoric rise to success the previous year. He was rather disappointed. He had, he says, 'been in the habit, for years, of objecting to the artificial style of the actors lately in vogue', and had hoped that in Kean he would see all that was 'natural and desirable in theatrical representation'. But even Kean in *Richard III* appeared 'nothing but a first-rate actor of the ordinary, stagy class, and to start only occasionally into passages of truth and originality'. Hunt has a long and interesting analysis of the artificial and the natural styles, and complains that Kean

> dealt out his syllables, and stood finely, and strutted at the set off of a speech, just as other well-received performers do; and he is much farther gone in stage trickery than we supposed him to be, particularly in the old violent contrasts when delivering an equivoque, dropping his voice too consciously from a serious line to a sly one, and fairly putting it to the house as a good joke.

Here he is complaining that the actor seemed to be standing somewhat outside the role, nudging the audience into noticing his artistry. But at other times Kean had 'touches of nature' such as Hunt was hoping to find. He had a manner of 'rubbing his hands' when Richard thought that he was succeeding in his aims, which Hunt found proper to the character. This, and 'other gestures . . . and the turns of his countenance [tended] in a very happy manner to unite common life with tragedy—which is the great stage-desideratum'.[1]

This is a recurrent theme. Hunt recognized that tragic acting required a certain elevation, but demanded that it should be intermingled with the familiar. Reviewing Fanny Kemble's Juliet in 1830, he found that she played in

[1] Ibid., 112–14.

the regular conventional tragic style, both in voice and manner, which was maintained with little variation the whole evening, and which has certainly left an impression on our minds that this young lady is entirely an artificial performer ... She wanted real passion throughout, and variety of feeling.[1]

Hunt's *bête noire* among the greatest actors of his time was John Philip Kemble; and long after Edmund Kean's *début*—indeed, in the last stages of Kean's career—he wrote a comparison of Kemble and Kean which sums up his ideas on this head, as well as showing that over the years he came to feel much more favourably about Kean. He admits 'a certain merit of taste and what is called "classicality"' in Kemble. He admits the truth of Kemble's feeling that 'a certain elevation of treatment' was due to tragedy, but he finds that with him all was 'external and artificial ... It was not the man, but his mask.' Kean, on the other hand, 'the finest tragic actor we ever beheld', was full of passion. His

face is full of light and shade, his tones vary, his voice trembles, his eye glistens, sometimes with withering scorn, sometimes with a tear: at least he can speak as if there were tears in his eyes, and he brings tears into those of other people.[2]

This distinction between the natural and the artificial is one that Hunt frequently makes; predictably, his preference is always for the natural.

This attitude towards acting is paralleled by Hunt's views on Shakespeare's plays. Often he takes their greatness as understood, but he has a number of panegyrics on Shakespeare's genius. He recognizes the impersonality of the dramatist's art:

The difficulty of getting at the real opinions of dramatic writers is notorious ... there is no more reason to imagine that he thought with *Iago* than that he did with *Falstaff*, or *Romeo*, or *Sir Andrew Aguecheek*. The character thought like itself, and that was enough for him.[3]

[1] Archer, 148.
[2] Ibid., 222–6.
[3] Houtchens, 82.

Again we observe the Romantic emphasis upon character. Hunt was writing in 1814. In the community of ideas to which I referred, it is interesting to find that this is essentially the view expressed three years later by Hazlitt in his lecture on 'Shakespeare and Milton': Shakespeare 'was the least of an egotist that it was possible to be. He was nothing in himself; but he was all that others were . . .'[1] And Keats, who heard Hazlitt's lecture, is nevertheless in some ways closer to Hunt in his letter of 27 October 1818 to Richard Woodhouse: 'the poetical character . . . has no self . . . It has as much delight in conceiving an Iago as an Imogen.'

A nineteenth-century phenomenon in relation to Shakespeare's characters is the adulation given to his women. Whereas until the time of Sir Walter Scott it was conventional to praise Beaumont and Fletcher above Shakespeare for their women characters, it was, wrote Terence Spencer in an essay on 'Shakespeare and the Noble Woman',[2] 'Coleridge's great discovery (which was exploited throughout the nineteenth century) that Shakespeare's women-characters were remarkable in that you felt like marrying them'. Shelley spoke of

> A wonder of this earth,
> Where there is little of transcendent worth—
> Like one of Shakespeare's women.
>
> (*Julian and Maddalo*, ll. 590–92)

And Leigh Hunt joined in this chorus, particularly in his later writings. In 1830 he has a whole paragraph of exclamations about them—'How poor do the women of almost all other dramatic poets (which they intend to be attractive or seducing) appear by the side of them! How unlovely their virtues, how vicious and unvoluptuous their love!' In the following year he is moved to rhetorical questions instead of exclamations: 'What notion of sweetness can be too great for such a character as Imogen? What

---

[1] *Lectures on the English Poets* (1818); an extract reprinted in *Shakespeare Criticism*, ed. D. Nichol Smith (1916), 305–19: 306.

[2] *Shakespeare Jahrbuch* (West) 97 (1966), 49–62.

perfect love and ingenuousness ought we not to look for in a Desdemona? What an union of cordiality with court shrewdness in Rosalind?'[1] and so on. No wonder he often found that actresses could not measure up to his expectations.

A curious sidelight on Hunt's views about the women characters is his interest in their legs. In Hunt's time ladies' legs were far less frequently displayed in public, or indeed anywhere other than in the most intimate surroundings, than now. Even on the stage, actresses normally wore long dresses—except, of course, when they were playing what were known as breeches roles. Shakespeare's disguised heroines, such as Viola and Rosalind, were popular partly for this reason. Hunt's comments suggest a natural attraction combined with a degree of that pre-Victorian prudishness which is the obverse of the Regency image. When Mrs Jordan played Rosalind, 'you admire the shape of her leg'; but Mrs Henry Siddons was even better because you admired her with 'a chastened feeling, you love the very awkwardness with which she wears her male attire, and you are even better pleased with her shape because you are left to fancy it'. Rather more than legs seems to have been on potential display when Miss Meadows played Ariel: 'We very much admired the air of modesty which this young lady preserved in a dress necessarily light and thin.' That was in 1807. By 1820 he was somewhat less concerned about modesty. Of Miss Tree's Viola, 'we must be allowed to say that her leg is the very prettiest leg we ever saw on the stage'. And he goes into analytical detail:

It is not at all like the leg which is vulgarly praised even in a man, and which is doubly misplaced under a lady—a bit of balustrade turned upside down; a large calf, and an ankle only small in proportion. It is a right feminine leg, delicate in foot, trim in ankle, and with a calf at once soft and well-cut, distinguished and unobtrusive. . . . It is impossible not to be struck, as an Irishman would say, with a leg like this. It is fit for a statue; still fitter for where it is.

[1] Archer, 183–4, 204.

The rest of the performance was less satisfactory. Ten years later he was still remembering Miss Tree's legs, in spite of the competition offered by the 'light smartness' of Miss Taylor's.[1]

A more general virtue in Shakespeare which rouses Hunt to rhetorical panegyric is his humanity. Comparing *The Merchant of Venice* with *The Jew of Malta*, he finds that 'up rose Shakspeare in the complete wisdom of his humanity'; and he apostrophizes him with full Romantic fervour: 'Blessings on thy memory, thou divinest of human beings . . .', continuing in a single rhapsodic sentence of over 200 words.[2]

But when it came to particular plays, Hunt was not always blindly adoring. Although he defended *King John* against Dr Johnson's strictures in a manner to which his editors apply the term 'romantic idolatry', other history plays, now more highly valued, were less to his taste. Reviewing *Henry IV*, Part One, in 1830, he wrote, 'the historical plays of Shakspeare certainly do not tell, as they used to do', though this one was at least partly redeemed by the character of Falstaff. *Henry V* pleased him still less: 'It is not a good acting play—at least not for these times.' His excuse on Shakespeare's behalf is that the play 'was written to please the uninformed subjects of a despotic government two hundred years ago, and as it comprises little of the everlasting humanity that fills most of the plays of Shakspeare, it falls flat on the ears of an audience in these times of popular spirit!'[3] No doubt Hunt's radical political opinions influenced his assessment of the history plays. Nor was he entirely sympathetic with the comedies. The improbabilities of *The Comedy of Errors* were too much for him; and in 1811 he found *Twelfth Night* 'perhaps the last in rank of Shakspeare's more popular dramas'. However, when he saw Frederick Reynolds's heavily adapted musical version in 1820—the one that displayed Miss Tree's legs so satisfactorily—he wrote a little panegyric on it: 'What a good-natured play was not this, altogether, to close his dramas with! for *Twelfth Night* was the

---

[1] On Mrs Jordan and Mrs H. Siddons: *Performers*, 209; Miss Meadows, ibid., Appendix, 32; Miss Tree: Houtchens, 228; Miss Taylor: Archer, 182.

[2] Houtchens, 197–8.

[3] Ibid., 301; Archer, 185, 179–80.

last work of Shakspeare.'[1] (In this opinion, he was simply following Malone.)

It cannot be claimed that Hunt shows any strongly Coleridgean
concern for the organic quality of Shakespeare's art. Admittedly,
he joins in the protests, increasingly common at this time, against
the continuing use in the theatre of the most flagrant adaptations,
such as the Dryden–Davenant *Tempest* (which he found morally
objectionable), Tate's *King Lear*, and Garrick's *Romeo and Juliet*.
But he was tolerant of other alterations, such as Reynolds's
musical versions of *The Comedy of Errors* and *Twelfth Night*; and
he mentions with no apparent consciousness of its impropriety
that in *As You Like It* Miss Taylor, as Rosalind, 'sang the cuckoo-
song with great good taste and effect, closing the stanzas well, . . .
and was ardently encored in it'. Clearly this was in a much
adapted version. Hunt's reviews do not suggest a serious concern
for over-all interpretation. He shows some signs of the interest
in the beginnings of the movement to present the plays with an
historical accuracy that would be educative as well as effective. Of
Kemble's *Julius Caesar* in 1812 he writes that 'an impression is left
upon us of Roman manners and greatness, of the appearance as
well as intellect of Romans, which to a young mind in particular
must furnish an indelible picture for the assistance of his studies'.
This seems a prim view of a notably spectacular production. He
remarks of *Henry IV*, Part One (in 1830) that

> we must dress up the historical play with plumes, and decora-
> tions, and real costume, in order to amuse the eye, because the
> other interest languishes. And we dress it very well, yet it
> languishes still.

And he observes that the scenery of *As You Like It* was

> very beautiful. When we did not like any actor who was
> speaking, *we took a walk in it*; and found ourselves in the midst
> of glades and woods, 'and alleys leading inward far'.[2]

---

[1] Houtchens, 327–9, 41, 231.
[2] Archer, 183; Houtchens, 65; Archer, 185, 184.

But in general Hunt's interest centres firmly on the actors, and on the problems of performers interpreting particular roles. This reflects both the theatrical and the intellectual fashions of his time. This was an actors' rather than a directors' theatre. Audiences hoped above all to be impressed and thrilled by great individual performers. Theatre-goers were connoisseurs of acting, seeing the great classic roles played by a variety of actors and avidly comparing the 'points' that they made. That which surrounded the leading actors was, in most theatres, a matter of comparative indifference. Only a few managers, Kemble among them, were beginning that process of reform in the over-all staging of plays which was to lead to the carefully managed productions of Samuel Phelps, Charles Kean, and Henry Irving, and finally to the directors' theatre as we know it today. The emphasis on star actors is itself a manifestation of Romanticism, with its fascination with individual personality.

Hunt had a keen sense of the difficulty experienced by actors in the attempt to encompass the full range of Shakespeare's major roles. This emerges strongly from his comparison (1819) of Edmund Kean and Macready as Richard III. He found that Kean's portrayal has 'more of the seriousness of conscious evil in it, the other [Macready's] of the gaiety of meditated success'. And he continues:

> If these two features in the character of *Richard* could be united by any actor, the performance would be a perfect one: but when did the world ever see a perfect performance of a character of Shakspeare's? When did it ever see the same *Macbeth*'s good and ill nature work truly together, the same *King John* looking mean with his airs of royalty, the same *Hamlet* the model of a court and the victim of melancholy? . . . The union of such a variety of tones of feeling as prevails in the great humanities of Shakspeare seems as impossible to be found in an actor, as the finest musical instrument is insufficient to supply all the effect of a great writer for a band.[1]

This theme recurs. As early as 1807, he had said,

[1] Houtchens, 220.

The character of Hamlet ... seems beyond the genius of the present stage, and I do not see that its personification will be easily attained by future stages, for its actor must unite the most contrary as well as the most assimilating powers of comedy and tragedy, and to unite these powers in their highest degree belongs to the highest genius only.[1]

Twenty-three years later, in 1830, he says something very similar in reviewing Macready's Hamlet:

We never yet saw a Hamlet on the stage, nor do we expect to see one. It is a character, though quite in nature, made up of too many qualities to be represented by any but a Hamlet himself. ... We have seen parts of Hamlet represented, but we never saw the whole.

And he goes on to discuss 'what Hamlet was' in a little character-sketch in line with many other examples of this kind of writing. (One could make a little anthology of character-sketches from Hunt's criticism.)

But more often than offering a self-contained sketch of an important character, Hunt tends to discuss the character in terms of the problems that it poses for the actor. This results in passages of analytical criticism which can be genuinely illuminating. For example, finding that Macready was sometimes too noisy as Hamlet, he excepts one loud passage:

His most warrantable loudness (indeed there it is desirable, because Hamlet is bullying his own indecision into action) was where he makes the stab through the arras, crying out 'Dead for a ducat!'[2]

That Hamlet is here 'bullying his own indecision into action' is a good perception. And sometimes Hunt passes from observation of the way a character is portrayed to generalized remarks about human behaviour which one imagines might still be valuable to actors studying certain roles. He has such a passage on Cassio's

[1] Archer, 87.
[2] Ibid., 161–3.

drunkenness. He praises Charles Kemble for the way that he makes Cassio's remorse appear

> so much the stronger from his inability to rid himself of the debauch which he abhors. There is no actor who imitates this defect with such a total want of affectation. All the other performers wish to be humorous drunkards, and by this error they cannot help showing a kind of abstract reasoning which defeats their purpose. They play a hundred antics with legs which a drunkard would be unable to lift, they make a thousand grimaces which the jaws of a drunkard could not attempt from mere want of tone; they roll about from place to place, though his whole strength is exerted to command his limbs; they wish, in short, to appear drunk, when the great object of a drunkard is to appear sober.[1]

There is a curious echo of this in an anecdote told in F. W. Hawkins's *Life of Edmund Kean* (1869, ii.360),

> . . . he was asked by a friend when he studied? Indicating a man on the other side of the room, who was very much intoxicated, but who was labouring to keep up an appearance of sobriety, he replied, 'I am studying now. I wish some of my Cassios were here. They might see that, instead of rolling about in the ridiculous manner they do, the great secret of delineating intoxication is the endeavour to stand straight when it is impossible to do so.'

Hunt's interest in individual character has a natural corollary in the prominence he gives to particular actors. It is significant that the only volume he himself published about the theatre is called *Critical Essays on the Performers of the London Theatres*. Each essay is about a particular actor; indeed, Hunt tells us in his Preface that his original plan was to write an essay about each and every actor on the list of the only two 'legitimate' theatres in London, Covent Garden and Drury Lane, and that 'it was not till the tragic section had been printed that I discovered the nameless multitude which this plan would have compelled me to individualize'. He hoped to

[1] Ibid., 111.

excite 'an honourable ambition in the actors, who have hitherto been the subjects of mere scandal, or at best of the most partial levity'. He hoped, in other words, by taking them seriously to encourage them to take themselves seriously. He defends the art of the actor by saying that 'If the knowledge of ourselves be the height of wisdom, is that art contemptible which conveys this knowledge to us in the most pleasing manner?' (It is rather touching, in the light of the present enterprise, that Hunt ends his Preface by saying that 'Upon so perishable a subject I cannot enjoy the hope of talking to other times.')[1] Many of his reviews, too, as I have suggested, centre firmly on the performance of the leading actor or actress. Their interest is, therefore, commensurate with our interest in the actors about whom he is writing. His notices of forgotten actors may have incidental interest in relation to the play in which they performed or because of the vigour of the prose in which Hunt discusses them. His notices of actors who continue to hold the attention of posterity are part of the reason they do so, an essential aspect of the record.

Of all the performers of his lengthy career as a theatre-goer, the one who achieved the most unanimous chorus of praise is the great Sarah Siddons, Sir Joshua Reynolds's 'Tragic Muse'. Her career was well advanced by the time that Hunt began going to the theatre, in 1800, and she officially retired in 1812. She was regarded as rather prudish (exceptionally, for actors in those days), and in view of what I wrote about 'breeches parts', it is interesting to read that 'she jibbed at the breeches in Rosalind, appearing in a costume which was that neither of a man nor of a woman, and extremely unbecoming'. Hunt's *Critical Essay* on her begins, 'To write a criticism on Mrs Siddons is to write a panegyric, and a panegyric of a very peculiar sort, for the praise will be true.' He praises her for absorption in her roles: 'Mrs Siddons has the air of never being the actress.' He finds that she has a power of which he often deplores the absence in other performers: the power to balance exactly the expression of human nature with the technical skill of the actor: she could seem natural while most powerfully projecting her art. Thus, in a later review of her Volumnia, he

[1] The Preface is reprinted in Archer, xxxvii–xlii.

writes, 'Mrs Siddons knows when to lift her countenance into commanding majesty, and when to fall into the familiarity of domestic ease.' (Yet in his *Autobiography*, written long afterwards, he admits to feeling that even in her 'something of too much art was apparent'.) The late date of Hunt's criticism means that when he writes of her it is usually in retrospect. He decided not to attend her farewell performance, but wrote an essay on the occasion, praising her Queen Katherine, Constance, and Lady Macbeth as 'almost perfect pieces of acting'. She excelled in portraying 'regality and conscious dignity', and

> it was in *Queen Katherine* that this dignity was seen in all its perfection; never was lofty grief so equally kept up, never a good conscience so nobly prepared, never a dying hour so royal and so considerate to the last. That was a beautiful touch with which she used to have her chair and cushions changed, during the wearisome pain of her resting body! And her cheek too against the pillow![1]

Here Hunt is praising touches of the nature which he found all too lacking in the performances of Mrs Siddons's distinguished brother, John Philip Kemble, about whom he is often remarkably and extendedly rude. Kemble, he says, should study such effects, and

> not the clap-provoking frivolities of ending every speech with an energetic dash of the fist, or of running off the stage after a vehement declamation, as if the actor was in haste to get his pint of wine.

When a role demanded the familiar touch, Kemble was—still Mr Kemble, as in Coriolanus's lines:

> I will go wash:
> And when my face is fair, you shall perceive
> Whether I blush or no.

[1] *Oxford Companion to the Theatre*, ed. Phyllis Hartnoll (3rd edn., 1967), s.v. Siddons, Sarah; Archer, 11, 13; *Performers*, Appendix, 6; *Autobiography*, 166; Houtchens, 72.

The word *fair* might positively have been measured by a stop-watch: instead of being a short monosyllable, it became a word of tremendous elongation. We can describe the pronunciation by nothing else than by such a sound as *fay-er-r-r*. Luckily for our fastidious, or as Mr Kemble would say, our *fastijjus* ears, we had no opportunity of hearing *bird* for *beard*; but it was in vain to expect any repose in orthöepy, when Mr Kemble had gotten such a word as *Aufidius* to transmogrify. This he universally called *Aufijjus*, like a young lady who talks of her *ojus* lover, or the *ojus* month of November. The name too of *Coriolanus* is divided by Mr Kemble with syllabical precision into five distinct sounds, though the general pronunciation, as well as Shakspeare himself, shortens the *rio* into one syllable, as in the word *chariot*: the alteration is of no effect, but to give a stiffness to what is already too stiff, and to render many of the poet's lines harsh and unmetrical.

Hunt seems to have felt strongly about Kemble's faults of pronunciation, which he ascribes to misplaced pedantry, and is unmercifully scornful about them on several occasions. He praised him in some roles, especially Prospero, but admits in his *Autobiography* that he thought him overrated: 'He was no more to be compared to his sister, than stone is to flesh and blood.'[1]

Probably the greatest male tragic actor about whom Hunt wrote was Edmund Kean, before whom, says Hunt, Kemble faded, 'like a tragedy ghost'. When Hunt saw him first, as Richard III, he was disappointed, probably because he had expected to find him the very antithesis of Kemble, whom he so much disliked. But he was profoundly moved by Kean's Othello, which he summed up as 'the masterpiece of the living stage'. He has interesting and touching notices of some of Kean's late performances, when some, but far from all, of the old magnetism had gone. It is sad to find him regretting, in 1831, that audiences do not applaud Kean as they once had:

Their shouts do not leap forth, as they used to do, at every turn and bidding of his genius, and we could not help thinking last

[1] Archer, 15–16, 114–15; *Autobiography*, 194.

night that some of his very finest passages met with a very ill and a very *ungrateful* reception, and that he felt it; and was the worse for it.[1]

While Leigh Hunt's over-all estimates of leading actors offer valuable evidence to the stage historian, perhaps the most striking passages of his theatre criticism in relation to Shakespeare's plays are those in which he describes and comments on the way particular actors handled specific, limited areas of the texts. In the best of these he reveals, along with an analytical capacity on which I have already commented, a sensitive response both to the sound of the lines and to visual effects of appearance, stage business, and the like. On speaking, for instance, he has an excellent close analysis of Fanny Kemble's delivery of Juliet's lines beginning 'Come, gentle night', which he finds that she treated far too solemnly rather than in the manner he feels to be appropriate,

> with a joyous tone throughout; with an undiminished hilarity; with her heart dancing in her eyes; nay, even with an enthusiastic pacing down the stage lamps, looking the audience rapturously in the face, as if she breathed out her soul to the air and to all nature.[2]

He is fine on Macready's handling of King John's last moments, and on a passage in Charles Mayne Young's Macbeth:

> His apostrophe to the imaginary dagger was impressive, but it wanted, what I never saw given to it yet, a variety of countenance approaching to delirium; and he spoke its first lines with his face turned away from *Duncan's* chamber door *directly toward* the side scenes: this appears to me an erroneous position: his face should at least have been a three-quarter one, for to give a most impassioned expression a profile only, except in cases which absolutely require it, is to cheat the audience of the full fancy of the scene.

[1] *Autobiography*, 193; Houtchens, 202; Archer, 227–8.
[2] Archer, 157.

Here Hunt shows himself to have that connoisseur's appreciation of the finer points of acting which must have inspired many of his contemporaries in their frequent revisits to a small number of classical plays; and in describing another moment of the same performance he shows a knowledge of traditional stage business:

> The imprecatory action of lifted arms with which he repulsed the ghost off the stage, according to custom, at that passage 'Hence horrible shadow! Unreal mockery hence!' was too violent and dictatorial.[1]

Understandably, some of Hunt's best writing is evoked by performances which particularly excited him, and I should like to quote two of these, both about Edmund Kean. The first refers to his death scene as Richard III, which must stand with Mrs Siddons's sleep-walking scene, in *Macbeth*, as one of the most powerful of all passages of Romantic acting. After seeing one of Kean's late performances, in 1831, Hunt wrote

> the crowning point was the look he gave Richmond, after receiving the mortal blow. This has been always admired; but last night it appeared to us that he made it longer and therefore more ghastly. He stood looking the other in the face, as if he was already a disembodied spirit, searching him with the eyes of another world; or, as if he silently cursed him with some new scorn, to which death and its dreadful knowledge had given him a right.[2]

Finally a description of Kean in his prime which, perhaps more than any other passage in Hunt's criticism, gives one a sense of feeling what it was like to be there. It is from a review of *Timon of Athens* (1816).

> *Timon*, digging in the woods with his spade, hears the approach of military music; he starts, waits its approach sullenly, and at last in comes the gallant *Alcibiades* with a train of splendid soldiery. Never was scene more effectively managed. First, you

---

[1] Ibid., 193–5; Houtchens, 22–3.
[2] Archer, 202.

heard a sprightly quick march playing in the distance; Kean started, listened, and leaned in a fixed and angry manner on his spade, with frowning eyes, and lips full of the truest feeling, compressed but not too much so; he seemed as if resolved not to be deceived, even by the charm of a thing inanimate; the audience were silent; the march threw forth its gallant note nearer and nearer; the Athenian standards appear, then the soldiers come treading on the scene with that air of confident progress which is produced by the accompaniment of music; and at last, while the squalid misanthrope still maintains his posture and keeps his back to the strangers, in steps the young and splendid *Alcibiades*, in the flush of victorious expectation. It is the encounter of hope with despair.[1]

At least in passages like this, surely. Leigh Hunt can 'enjoy the hope of talking to other times'.

[1] Houtchens, 138.

VII

The Plays of Gordon Bottomley

KENNETH MUIR

No verse play written by a poet in the eighteenth and nineteenth centuries has remained in the professional repertory. There have been occasional performances of *The Cenci* and of a few other plays but, theatrically speaking, they are dead. Yet there have been several occasions when a revival of poetic drama seemed to be on the cards—at the time of Talfourd's stodgy successes, when Irving acted in Tennyson's *Becket*, and when the author of *Paolo and Francesca* was strangely hailed as Shakespeare's heir. When Yeats began to write plays there seemed to be a greater chance of success. His themes, whether political or mythological, were all relevant to an Irish audience; he had a theatre in which he could painfully learn his craft as a playwright; he was to become a great poet; and he realized that Elizabethan drama was not a suitable model for a modern dramatist.

Yeats was followed in England by several poets to whom drama was no more than a sideline. Binyon, for example, wrote a number of verse plays,[1] but his chief work was a translation of Dante; and Masefield, who wrote poetic plays in a variety of styles,[2] was mainly famous for his narratives in verse and prose. To Gordon Bottomley, however, drama was not a sideline: he was writing plays for fifty years. Since he was confined to the country for

---

[1] *Boadicea* is the best of these.

[2] *Good Friday* and *Philip the King* in rhymed verse; *A King's Daughter* in blank verse; *The Tragedy of Nan* and *The Faithful* in poetic prose.

Grateful acknowledgements are due to Roger Lancelyn Green, Bottomley's literary executor, for permission to quote passages from letters and plays, to the Huntington Library where I was able to consult a collection of unpublished letters, to John Dixon Hunt, who lent me family letters, memoranda, and copies of *A Stage for Poetry* and *A Note on Poetry and the Stage*, and to the Bodley Head and Messrs Constable and Co. None of Bottomley's plays is now in print.

many years by ill-health, maintaining contact with artists and
poets mainly through correspondence, his devotion to drama was
the more remarkable. Nearly all his plays are one-acters, and this
meant that they were crowded out of professional repertoires;
only towards the end of his life, when he was commissioned to
write *The Acts of St Peter* for performance in Exeter Cathedral,
did he attempt a longer play. The shortness of most of his
work was partly due to the state of his health. He described
how he composed *King Lear's Wife* in his head, twelve lines at a
time:[1]

> In the end I could do as much as twenty lines a day if I did not
> forget to be cautious. By the end of the Summer of 1913 I had
> finished *King Lear's Wife*: throughout that fragmentary, inter-
> rupted process of composition the theme had held me intently.

In the account of his work written at the end of his life, *A Stage
for Poetry* (1948), Bottomley divided his output into two periods:
plays for the theatre outworn, and plays for a theatre unborn.
This division exaggerates the difference between the two kinds,
for the early plays, up to and including *Britain's Daughter* (1920),
were never really designed for the professional stage, though two
of them had professional performances in London; and *Kate
Kennedy*, one of his last plays, is a light comedy which could easily
have been a popular success. Nevertheless, as we shall see, there
were good reasons for Bottomley's division.

He regarded himself as Yeats's disciple. In 1921 he wrote to him
as 'the unapproachable master of us all in this craft'. But whereas
Yeats could draw on Irish mythology in a deliberate attempt to
foster a national consciousness, Bottomley has no such need or
resource. His sources were very varied: folklore in *Midsummer Eve*,
Icelandic saga in *The Riding to Lithend*, legendary British history
(*King Lear's Wife* and *Britain's Daughter*); and later he went to
Scottish legends and history. His plays were generally set in a past
which had little relation to a modern audience; and only occasionally, as in the anti-war speeches of *Britain's Daughter*, written just

---

[1] *Poems and Plays*, ed. C. C. Abbott (1953), 15.

after the First World War, do we feel that Bottomley was directly addressing a contemporary audience:[1]

> Shall I waste my blood as you waste others' blood?
> If men must fight for Britain, women must live for Britain:
> But your mother and her brood, the ruling women,
> The mad fighting fools, who have poured us out
> In their pride, in their high-minded magnanimity,
> With noble gestures of their souls, with priceless passions,
> Let them be brought to lamentation.

Bottomley's later plays—plays for a theatre unborn—were influenced even more by Yeats's example, both by *Four Plays for Dancers* and by the Nōh plays which inspired them. The folding and unfolding of the curtain by a chorus, a device often used by Bottomley in his chamber plays, was avowedly copied from Yeats.

The best of the early plays was undoubtedly *The Riding to Lithend*, a remarkable recreation of the spirit of the 'fierce saga' on which it is based, written in spare and eloquent verse. It would, however, be difficult to stage, partly because of the fight at the end, and partly because of the primitive passions of the main characters which audiences would find unsympathetic. Hallgerd boasts early in the play:[2]

> I am a hazardous desirable thing,
> A warm unsounded peril, a flashing mischief,
> A divine malice, a disquieting voice:
> Thus I was shapen, and it is my pride
> To nourish all the fires that mingled me.
> I am not long moved, I do not mar my face,
> Though men have sunk in me as in a quicksand.
> Well, death is terrible. Was I not worth it?

She refuses to help her hard-pressed husband, Gunnar, by letting him use her hair for his bow-string; and she speaks of the rapture of killing:[3]

[1] 'Gruach' and 'Britain's Daughter' (1921), 82.
[2] *Poems and Plays*, 103.   [3] Ibid., 125.

> It is so mighty and beautiful and blithe
> To watch a man dying—to hover and watch.

It has been noticed that despite Bottomley's peaceful life, and the literary inspiration of nearly all his plays, they contain a great deal of violence. He seems to have agreed with Masefield, another gentle soul, who said in the preface to *The Tragedy of Nan* that the heart of life is laid bare only in the agony and exultation of dreadful acts. In *The Crier by Night*, Bottomley's first play, and in *Midsummer Eve*, the central characters die; in the third play Laodice murders Danae; there is a murder in *King Lear's Wife*, torture in *Britain's Daughter*, a massacre in *Towie Castle*, in *The Singing Sands* and in *Dunaverty*; Marsaili weeps for the brutal murder of her three children, and Ardvorlich's wife finds her brother's head on the dining table.

The strength of *The Riding to Lithend* can be appreciated by contrast with another early play, *Midsummer Eve*, in which three girls, according to an old superstition, look for the faces of their future husbands. Despite some fine verse, the play is spoilt by some silly names—Dame Stir-Wench, Mam Pantry, Mam Patch-Waist, Mother Dish-Clout—and even more by the high-faluting language put into the mouths of the chief characters, milkmaids and kitchen-wenches:[1]

> Humbly we measure ourselves by all we see,
> We feel uneasily yet willingly
> Each thing that happens may happen to us too,
> And we are cheated of each grief unsuffered—
> Yea, ever we interrogate decay
> To know our own duration; we must touch
> Each lovesome thing lest it or we should fade,
> Until the arching quiver of contact reaches
> And makes us conscious where we can be lovesome.

Bottomley's first real success was *King Lear's Wife* which was published in *Georgian Poetry* and won immediate recognition. It was followed after the war by *Gruach*, a play about the early life of

[1] *'King Lear's Wife' and Other Plays* (1920), 161.

Lady Macbeth. A question often asked about these plays was the extent to which Bottomley was relying on their associations with Shakespeare: would they be good plays if the characters were named Queenie and Macleod? They would still be interesting plays, but Bottomley was quite legitimately relying on our knowledge of *King Lear* and *Macbeth*. The plays are not indirect dramatic criticism but an attempt to guess at the early lives of famous Shakespearian characters. *King Lear's Wife* depends a great deal on our memories of Shakespeare's play, almost as if it had been revised by Goneril. Her character, with her attachment to her dying mother, her resentment of her father's unfaithfulness, her prowess as a hunter, and her ruthless murder of the King's mistress, prepare the way for the brave, unscrupulous character of Shakespeare's play; but her Diana-like characteristics make her infatuation with Edmund an improbable development, and she is completely without hypocrisy. Regan does not appear; and Cordeil's whining voice is heard only off-stage. She is disliked by her mother, who became pregnant with her only to keep Lear from other women:[1]

> Because a woman gives herself for ever
> Cordeil the useless had to be conceived
> (Like an after-thought that deceives nobody)
> To keep her father from another woman.

Such a child could hardly develop into one who redeemed nature from the general curse. Lear is lecherous and mean. He refuses to allow an emerald to be powdered, although assured by a physician that it might save the Queen's life. His lecherous behaviour may have been suggested by Gloucester's behaviour in the early years of his marriage: there is no trace of the capacity for suffering which is apparent in Shakespeare's Lear. But the liberties Bottomley takes with the well-known story are no more than those taken by Euripides, Racine, Sartre and Anouilh with Aeschylean and Sophoclean characters.

[1] *Poems and Plays*, 142.

King Lear's Wife was first performed at the Birmingham Repertory Theatre in 1915 and there was a matinée performance in 1916 at His Majesty's Theatre. *Gruach*, after Tyrone Guthrie's production in Glasgow, was performed with Sybil Thorndike in the title role, at St Martin's Theatre in 1924. Meanwhile *Britain's Daughter* had been produced by Robert Atkins at the Old Vic. These were the years when it seemed possible that Bottomley might consolidate these modest successes by writing more plays for the London stage. There were several reasons why this did not happen. First, there was a stark contrast between the enthusiasm of his fellow poets, and other critics, for the plays in print, and the response of dramatic critics to their performance. To John Drinkwater the plays were 'not to be excelled by anything that has been put on the English stage since the Elizabethans'; Lascelles Abercrombie hailed 'a renewal of the many-sided Elizabethan creativeness; the power of vivid exposition and organic structure, the command of subtle metre and profoundly symbolic imagery'; and *The Times Literary Supplement* declared that the dynamic quality of the plays could be fully realized only on the stage. But when the plays were seen on the stage, the reactions were much less favourable. There were complaints, for example, about the masterly ending of *King Lear's Wife*; and the critic of *The London Mercury* said that *Gruach* on the stage

> goes to pieces. Some of the language is too stilted to be spoken; some is so verbosely descriptive or picturesque that the actors are forced to gabble it; ... everything is too long; and finally, after the climax has been passed there is a long series of anti-climaxes that add nothing, and one of the most ineffective curtains ever seen on any stage.

This hostile account was partly due to the performance. Bottomley, while admiring Sybil Thorndike, said that the play would get only six rehearsals,[1]

---

[1] *Poet and Painter* (the correspondence between Gordon Bottomley and Paul Nash, 1910–46), ed. C. C. Abbott and A. Bertram (1955), 167. Bottomley was comparatively lucky: there was a professional performance of Masefield's *Pompey the Great* at Stratford-upon-Avon without a single rehearsal.

and poetry needs sixty; and then everybody will say that poetic drama is dead. But it is only the trade theatre that is dead, dead because it has learnt to exist without poetry.

Bottomley realized that part of the trouble was that the actors were not used to plays in verse:[1]

I never found a whole cast sympathetic to verse and skilled in its delivery. That may have been one reason why the journalist critics to a man found my verse unsuited to the theatre, and advised me to stick to poetry: but I believe now that the picture-frame theatre had so steadily diseducated them ... in the application of verse to the stage, that they had never understood or conceived that poetry could have a relationship to drama at all.

The Press, he told Paul Nash, 'doesn't know what to ask for from poetic drama, and can't usually think of anything but blaming the Tortoise for being slow'. Not unnaturally, Bottomley had a low opinion of the prominent dramatic critics of his time, including the 'definitely reactionary' Agate and Walkley, and Darlington who, in adjudicating a British Drama League competition, slated one team because they had chosen to perform 'a gloomy play—Mrs Lear.'[2]

---

[1] *A Stage for Poetry* (Kendal, 1948), 18. Bottomley did not condemn all English actors in this way. He spoke warmly of Ion Swinley as his Lear at Birmingham; he admired Edith Evans; and he said that Gielgud's first attempt at Shakespeare's Lear at the Old Vic 'was one of the grandest things I ever saw'. He thought that Ernest Milton and Marie Ney were great tragic players 'in an age that doesn't want them'. But on a visit to Stratford he found the plays difficult to follow because the verse was spoken so badly. A few years later, just before he died, he saw two Hamlets in a single day (Scofield and Helpmann) and commented on the latter that he was 'becoming a dangerous competitor to all the Oliviers and other so-and-so's of our generation'. On the same visit Bottomley was taken by Barry Jackson to a conference of Shakespearian scholars and remarked in a letter to K. Preston (31 August 1948): 'I have been saddened regularly to find how unsatisfactory and even contemptible to them English performances of Shakespeare are.'

[2] Another British Drama League adjudicator said that audiences liked to see pretty actresses and that therefore it was wrong to give the part of the medium in *The Words on the Window Pane* to an actress who was very plain.

The strongest reason, however, for Bottomley's failure to follow up the London productions of his plays was a performance of *Gruach* in November 1922 by the Scottish National Theatre Society:[1]

> I began to understand in Glasgow; for there I was learning all the time from the gifted young people with whom I was working. Their fine vowels and trained diction made listening a delight; the audience thought so too, and gave my verse the credit.

He told Paul Nash,[2]

> the Scotch voices are lovely, the Scotch players act with the intensity of people who are new to art and in a passion of love with it, and they get inside the psychology of my people as English players rarely do.

Soon afterwards John Masefield, who had also been impressed by the speakers of verse at Glasgow, started the Oxford Recitations—competitions for the speaking of verse in a way poets could approve—and he invited Bottomley not merely to be one of the judges, but also to write very short plays to be performed by the contestants. The first four duologues in *Scenes and Plays* (1929) were of this nature, and two of them, *A Parting* and *Sisters*, display a new power and poignancy, in verse that would only seem prosaic to the prosaic. The other plays in this volume were performed for the most part at Masefield's private theatre at Boar's Hill. This was designed for the work of contemporary poets (Binyon, Masefield, Yeats) as well as for revivals of Elizabethan plays. It helped to emancipate Bottomley from what he regarded as the tyranny of the ordinary modern theatre. Masefield's simple stage, on two levels with a balcony, and with a traverse curtain, had no scenery. This last factor made it less than ideal for Bottomley's work; for he liked to be thought of as the last of the pre-Raphaelites, he was a friend of Ricketts and Paul Nash, and he

---

[1] *A Stage for Poetry*, 19.
[2] *Poet and Painter*, 171.

paid very great attention to the settings and costumes of his plays, as we can see from *A Stage for Poetry*.

Nearly all the later plays[1] make use of a verse-speaking chorus, sometimes representing snow (*Ardvorlich's Wife*), sometimes winds and trees (*Culbin Sands*), sometimes mist (*Suilven and the Eagle*), and sometimes fishwives (*The White Widow*). In *A Note on Poetry and the Stage* (1944) Bottomley explained what he had been trying to do in his later plays, both in the use of the chorus and in his refusal to be confined to the use of blank verse:

> The blank verse of our dead theatre is no longer sufficient: every kind of verse form should find a place and a function in a live theatre, as they all did in the beginning—lyric measures in the chorus; narrative measures, and specific narrative poetry, in forwarding the development of the play's theme and in bridging and subsuming places in the story not easily capable of dramatic exhibition; and more metrical devices than the customary one (and even including stanzaic forms) in the essential poetic device of soliloquy, but equally in dialogue also.

Bottomley goes on to suggest that the function of the chorus can be usefully enlarged by depriving them of personal existence and using them as a substitute for scene painting, 'even to create the atmosphere in which characters exist and the play passes'.

In most of his 'chamber' plays, the plots are taken from Scottish legend: the action is distanced not merely by this fact but also by the framing of the main event by a lyrical chorus. There is virtually no narrative interest. We are informed by the chorus of the situation: that Lady Forbes and her children had been killed when Towie Castle was burned down on the orders of Adam Gordon; that a Spanish ship, infected with the plague, had anchored in Loch Leven; that Ardvorlich's wife, after seeing the head of her murdered brother on the table, had fled to the mountains and not been seen for months; in *Culbin Sands*, that while Alison had been in America her village had been covered by the sand; and that Marsaili's three children had been murdered before her eyes. In most cases the main action has taken place months or years before,

[1] See *Lyric Plays* (1932) and *Choric Plays and a Comedy* (1939).

and we are more concerned with memories of the past than with present action: Ardvorlich finds his wife and learns that she has borne a child during her period of madness in the mountains; and in *Fire at Callart* Mairi's lover arrives just in time to rescue her from the burning house. In three of the plays the theme is forgiveness of intolerable wrongs: Marsaili forgives the murderer of her three children; Adam Gordon is forgiven by the ghost of Jean Forbes, the girl he had spitted on his spear; and in *Dunaverty* the girl whose hands had been amputated is reconciled with the daughter of the man responsible.

The weakest of the plays is *Suilven and the Eagle* in which a mother follows an eagle to the top of a mountain in order to recover her baby from the kidnapper. Symbolically it contrasts Power and Maternal Determination, but it would strain the credulity of any audience. The incident is framed by various discussions—between the two peaks, between the peaks and the eagle, and between the chorus and the mother. The chorus consists of eight veiled women, representing the mountain mist. It is a lyrical recital rather than a play. There is a much more effective use of the chorus in *Culbin Sands*, where eight women represent the winds and six the trees. This is a metrical *tour-de-force*, with some exquisite sound effects. It creates an eerie atmosphere and, more effectively than narrative, it informs the audience of the covering of the village by the sand.

The theory behind the 'chamber' plays was expressed most clearly in a passage which might equally apply to some of the later plays of Yeats; Bottomley said that poetic drama is[1]

> not so much a representation of a theme as a meditation upon it or a distillation from it; its business is far less the simulation of life than the evocation and isolation for our delight of the elements of beauty and spiritual illumination in the perhaps terrible and always serious theme chosen.

There is no doubt that Bottomley did succeed in his aim. His meditations on the tragic events, whether expressed by the chorus

[1] *Poems and Plays*, 17.

or as part of the dialogue, are poetical and poignant. They are excellent to read, and when spoken by trained speakers of verse they can give genuine pleasure. Nevertheless one is bound to wonder whether the pleasure is genuinely dramatic, or if it is not the same kind of pleasure one would receive from a poetry recital. Stendhal, writing of the French tragedies being written at the beginning of the nineteenth century, remarked that the public 'loves to hear the recitation of lofty sentiments in fine verse' but that a truly dramatic pleasure is aroused in the theatre when we forget our surroundings and the medium and succumb, if only at moments, to the illusion. He added that 'one of the things which is most hostile to the birth of these moments of illusion is admiration for the beautiful verses of a tragedy'.[1] T. S. Eliot likewise expressed the hope that audiences would not realize that his plays were written in verse because the attitude of people listening to poetry is aesthetically reverent. Although Stendhal was anxious to have prose tragedies, and approved of Shakespeare because he thought that blank verse was nearer to prose than the rhymed alexandrines of Racine, and although Eliot proved himself wrong by his practice, since his most dramatically effective work is the most obviously poetical, yet there is a grain of truth in both pronouncements. When we watch a performance of *Macbeth*, the action is so gripping, we become so involved with the characters, that the poetry spoken by the actors, however magnificent, seems to be their natural speech. But in the type of play which Bottomley was advocating, the tragic events are so distanced—the murders of Marsaili's children and Jean Forbes—and we are so anaesthetized by the poetry of the choruses, that contemplation is substituted for drama.

Only one of these chamber plays is a comedy—*The Falconer's Lassie*—and it was presumably the success of this rather slight piece, and the writing of *The Acts of St Peter*, his first full-length play after twenty-four short ones, that led Bottomley to write *Kate Kennedy*, a spirited and delightful comedy of love set in medieval St Andrews, in which Kate changes clothes with her

[1] *Oeuvres completes de Stendhal*, ed. Victor del Litto and Ernest Abravanel, 50 vols. (Geneva, 1967-72), XXXVII. 8, 17.

student lover to take part in an innocent saturnalia. Some of Bottomley's friends suggested that he had moved away from his previous conceptions of drama and implied, perhaps, that he was compromising. He replied to W. Graham Robertson in January 1940:[1]

> It wasn't a change of heart that hatched my Kate; I have always believed that comedy (even poetic comedy) must come nearer to life as it is actually lived (even though it has a chorus as in Aristophanes) and must deal with individuals and idiosyncracies —not with types and universal qualities as tragedy does.

Everyone admired the heroine of this play and Bottomley was disappointed that only one reader appreciated the hero. He told Paul Nash,[2]

> You know, Beato Paolo, that you are like everyone else, and have fallen for my daughter Kate (though secretly)—in spite of looking down upon her aloofly. I am dejected: I expected you to say 'Yes Gordon . . . Isn't the girl a rather obvious charmer? The boy seems to me to be the one that is really well done— and, at that, far harder to do . . .'

It is natural for a poet to value most the successes which have been most difficult; but in fact both characters are admirably drawn. What Kate says of her lover exhibits her own charm and his:[3]

> O, I have seen
> You believed I could not know what I was doing;
> But I know more than you.
> He cannot understand what I want of him;
> But when he is bewildered, anxious, eager,
> He gives it to me sometimes, and is adorable
> In the sensitive harmony he creates between us.

Kate Kennedy is a delightful comedy, but almost too benign; for the old are wise and tolerant in the play and are not really an obstacle to the ultimate union of the lovers.

[1] Huntington Library.   [2] *Poet and Painter*, 262.   [3] *Kate Kennedy* (1945), 59.

A generation has passed since Gordon Bottomley died and, as his plays are all out of print, there is no sign of a revival of interest in his work. Yet it could be argued that the best of his plays have dated less than those of Auden and Isherwood and other dramatists of the thirties. He always appealed to a minority taste and never received adequate performances in London. Yet his plays were deservedly admired at drama festivals and in the more experimental little theatres.

Although Bottomley appealed more to fellow poets, including Edward Thomas and Robert Frost, and to readers of poetry, than he did to the ordinary theatre-going public, he was not a writer of closet-dramas. His plays, even the chamber plays, gain by being performed. This is partly due to his sense of dramatic structure. He was rightly annoyed with the critics who complained of the supposed anti-climaxes of *King Lear's Wife* and *Gruach*. The ending of the former, with two women preparing the corpse for burial, is grotesque but appropriate: its earthy realism, its talk of stealing, and its song of the louse leaving the corpse, link up with a reference in the first speech of the play to 'fumbling corpse-washers'; and in the middle of the scene Goneril comes in to wash the knife with which she has just murdered Gormflaith.

The second dramatic gift possessed by Bottomley was the ability to depict a wide range of characters, especially women. We never feel, as we do with some dramatists, that he writes from the point of view of a single character. We have continually to modify our views. We begin, for example, by sympathizing with Lear's wife, dying unloved and neglected; but when we hear what she says about Cordeil and of her frigidity, and when she incites Goneril to murder Gormflaith, our feelings change. There is a similar change with regard to Goneril.

Finally, by 1913 Bottomley had evolved a kind of blank verse which was not an imitation of Elizabethan verse, but which was recognizable as his own, which could be varied to suit the different characters, and which gave the illusion of natural speech.[1] In the later plays, where more varied verse forms are used, there is the

---

[1] There were a few lapses into poeticisms, as Bottomley realized when he saw the plays performed.

same insistence on natural speech, even in the incantatory choruses. Yet one play, written near the end of Bottomley's life, was in prose. *Deirdire* was based on Alexander Carmichael's translation from the Gaelic entitled *Deirdire and the Lay of the Children of Uisne*. Bottomley's play was accompanied by a translation into Gaelic by David Urquhart. Although we may disagree with Claude Colleer Abbott that

> this version of one of the world's most poignant stories need not fear comparison even with the plays of Yeats and Synge on the same theme,

Bottomley's choice of prose may perhaps indicate that he had come to realize that the distinction between verse and prose was not as important as he had once thought, when he had remonstrated with Clifford Bax for deserting verse, and that it was possible to have poetic plays in prose.